IMAGES
of America

CLOVIS

IN THE BEGINNING. Clovis was a budding trading center in the late 1800s, prior to the town's incorporation as a city February 27, 1912. Lumber was the primary business, with up to 200,000 board feet of fresh cut timber sent down a wooden flume each day from Shaver to the Clovis mill, which was located roughly where Clark Intermediate School and the Clovis Rodeo Grounds are today. The mill employed hundreds of men who created a need for food and lodging. There were several hotels and saloons here. By 1891, a railroad was running through the town that had been given the official name of Clovis, after prominent citizen Clovis Cole. Pictured at Fifth and Front Streets is a wagon of lumber ready to transport. The Byron Hotel and John E. Good mercantile can be seen in the background. (Clovis Museum.)

ON THE COVER: This 1922 image shows the corner of Fourth Street and Pollasky Avenue, the heart of the then 10-year-old city of Clovis. The dirt roads weaving through town were dotted with mercantiles, diners, social halls, churches, schools, and residences, while farms and ranches surrounded the region. Pictured is a wagon with a team of horses in front of the building housing the office of the *Clovis Tribune*, the first regular newspaper in town. Land sales were a booming business, and the building prominently displays a real estate office sign. This picture was taken just prior to Clovis receiving its first paved streets. The smoother surface was highly anticipated by those who had moved on from the horse and buggy to choose the automobile as their new primary source of transportation. (Gail William Forbes.)

IMAGES
of America

CLOVIS

Clovis Centennial Book Committee
John Wright, Patti Lippert Fennacy,
Sayre McFarlane Miller, Carol Wright,
Judith Preuss, and Tom Ebert

ARCADIA
PUBLISHING

Published by Arcadia Publishing
Charleston, South Carolina

Library of Congress Control Number: 2011927662

For all general information, please contact Arcadia Publishing:
Telephone 843-853-2070
Fax 843-853-0044
E-mail sales@arcadiapublishing.com
For customer service and orders:
Toll-Free 1-888-313-2665

Visit us on the Internet at www.arcadiapublishing.com

*To all who call Clovis home—from early pioneers to
residents today—thanks for making our community a
celebration of enduring stories and bold vision.*

CONTENTS

ACKNOWLEDGMENTS

This volume was made possible by the generous cooperation of many individuals and organizations.

Many published and unpublished works were consulted for historical information. The Fresno City and County Historical Society Archives, the Fresno County Public Library in downtown Fresno and its Clovis branch, the archives of the *Clovis Tribune* and the *Clovis Independent*, and the Special Collections Department of the Henry Madden Library, California State University, Fresno, proved to be rich depositories of Clovis history. Many of the published works are included in the bibliography of this volume. In addition to these works, a number of pamphlets, produced over time by various local groups, were consulted.

Individuals, too many to fully enumerate here, were also generous with their time, their historical recollections, their searches for historical photographs and materials, and their willingness to assist in the preservation of the history of our community. Some who must be acknowledged for their tireless assistance include Peg Bos, president of the Clovis–Big Dry Creek Historical Society; William Secrest Jr. of the Fresno County Public Library; John Reynolds, local historian; and Dan Guice, retired Clovis firefighter.

The members of the Clovis Centennial Book Committee who spent countless volunteer hours conducting research, collecting images, and writing this book are John Wright, retired Clovis city planning director; Carol Wright, CenterStage Clovis Community Theater president; Patti Lippert Fennacy, former *Clovis Independent* newspaper editor; Sayre McFarlane Miller, fifth-generation Clovis family farmer; Judith Preuss, lifelong Clovis resident and historian; and Tom Ebert, retired California State University, Fresno, librarian.

We encourage those interested in learning more about the rich history of Clovis to visit the Clovis–Big Dry Creek Historical Society Museum at 401 Pollasky Avenue in the heart of Old Town Clovis.

All proceeds generated from the sale of this book will be distributed to the Clovis Community Foundation (www.cloviscommunityfoundation.org), a nonprofit organization that supports culture, arts, and recreation projects in Clovis.

Unless otherwise noted, images in this book appear courtesy of the City of Clovis. Images provided by the Clovis–Big Dry Creek Historical Society Museum are credited as "Clovis Museum."

INTRODUCTION

A wheat farmer, an ambitious railroad man, entrepreneurial families, and visionary lumbermen are among the cast of characters who can be credited with the birth of Clovis, California, in the latter part of the 1800s. The city celebrates its centennial anniversary on February 27, 2012, but the city's roots began long before the 1912 date of incorporation.

Nestled in California's Central Valley adjacent to the majestic Sierra Nevada range, Clovis offered westward-bound pioneers a place to set up home. Land was in abundance, and the soil was fertile with possibilities. Posters promoting the Central Valley circulated in Europe and the eastern United States in 1870. Sponsored by land companies looking to sell 20-acre parcels in the area, the posters promised prosperity and prime farmland.

Clovis Cole's family was among the many enticed to make the westward move, and they relocated here from Indiana in 1873. Cole became a wheat farmer who eventually owned 40,000 acres in Fresno and Madera Counties. Among his first land purchases was 480 acres roughly in the area that is now Old Town Clovis. A budding town emerged on and around this property, including homesteads, ranches, and shops.

In 1891, Marcus Pollasky arrived and promoted the development of a railroad line that would connect the valley and travel across the Sierra. With his magnetic personality, he sought out investors and touted the economic boom the railroad would bring as goods could be transported to other markets. Cole signed on as a supporter, with visions of moving his wheat. He sold land for the railroad to Pollasky. The town and a train depot next to Cole's property would bear his first name, Clovis. According to local folklore, Cole's last name was not used because it would have sounded too similar to the rail line's coaling station.

In 1890, the Pineridge Flume and Irrigation Co. set out to build a 42-mile flume that would connect the wooded region near Shaver to a lumberyard in Clovis. Pineridge sold the uncompleted project to a group of investors who changed the name to Fresno Flume & Irrigation in 1891, and by 1894 the V-shaped flume was complete. At its peak, 200,000 board feet per day of rough lumber traveled down the waters of the flume to the Clovis mill.

The hub of the young town was roughly bordered by modern-day First to Fifth Streets and Hughes to Pollasky Avenues. Front Street, which is present-day Clovis Avenue, ran north to south, effectively bisecting the developing parcel. To the east of Front Street stretched the rail line, with the Clovis Depot located at Fourth Street and the lumberyard just a short distance south near Fifth Street. Shops offering goods and services lined the dusty dirt roads to the west of Front Street. Buildings were of varied heights and design, but each had a porch, a wooden sidewalk, and a place to tie up a horse.

The community opened its first school in 1895. Children from kindergarten through eighth grade met in the Southern Pacific warehouse for class until a permanent schoolhouse was constructed at Second Street and Pollasky Avenue in 1897. The first area high school opened in 1902 east of the railroad tracks between Fourth and Fifth Streets. Lee R. Brown was the school's only graduate that first year.

With visions of a growing town, property owners around the mill hired surveyor Ingvart Tielman (a.k.a Inyroot Trilman) to draft a map for Clovis's orderly growth. The town of about 500 people in 1905 grew to around 1,000 by 1910. Also growing were the nearby colonies—such as Garfield Colony, Temperance Colony, and Jefferson Colony—where families bought 20-acre parcels of land from developers to farm and build their homes.

By 1912, local businessmen became interested in incorporating Clovis into a city that collected taxes and provided public services. Voters approved incorporation. On February 27, 1912, the city of Clovis became official. Two months later, elections were held for a board of trustees. Two slates were presented, with one wanting to prohibit alcohol in town. By a vote of 168 to 83, the dry slate won. Lewis W. Gibson was named president of the Clovis Board of Trustees, the predecessor to today's Clovis City Council.

Clovis became a way of life as a sense of community enveloped the area. Social gatherings, ranging from school events to barn dances, unified citizens. The Clovis Women's Club organized a spring festival in 1914 to raise money to build a clubhouse. The festival—which brought area ranchers together to compete in mule-riding and calf-roping events—evolved to become the annual Clovis Rodeo that is still celebrated today.

For the next two decades, the community grew slowly but steadily. Modern amenities came to Clovis, including paved roads, sewers, telephone service, and police and fire departments. Rising above the challenges of world events such as the 1919 flu epidemic, World War I, and the Great Depression, Clovis citizens continued to improve their way of life. Dr. McMurtry established the Clovis Sanitarium and served the community for over half a century. Local fraternal organizations flourished and churches established congregations. Small town Clovis contributed to the war effort of World War II in monetary support and personal sacrifice.

In December 1959, a controversial decision—debated for years prior—occurred when voters approved bringing local school districts together with Clovis Union High School to form the Clovis Unified School District. Dr. Floyd Buchanan was named the district's first superintendent and would lead CUSD for the next 30 years as it developed into an award-winning, nationally recognized academic institution. The city's population of around 5,000 in 1960 more than doubled in the next decade to 13,586, in part because of the highly acclaimed district that drew people to live within its boundaries.

To accommodate the rapid growth and maintain the well-loved, small-town feel of Clovis, the city made a shift in the form of city government in 1971. The city hired a professional city manager and department administrators to address the wide range of issues facing the growing city. Over the next two decades, plans for construction of a new hospital, two new high schools, a regional shopping center, and revitalization of downtown Clovis were seminal issues.

In 1992, a General Plan for the city's future was adopted that focused on preserving Old Town Clovis as the center of the city and maintaining the central value of the community family. Schools, community organizations, businesses, and citizens worked together to establish the "Clovis Way of Life." The housing boom of the following decades further expanded the community, and Clovis began to be an address of distinction in the Central San Joaquin Valley.

Today, as Clovis looks to pass the 100,000 population mark, the city now includes 23 square miles. The community continues to welcome newcomers, as it did when our forefathers came to settle the land as farmers, entrepreneurs, and lumbermen. And while many things in the landscape of the town have changed, one thing remains the same. Those who call Clovis home remain loyal to a small-town way of life, where family, friends, and community are top priority.

One

THE EARLY DAYS

PRE-1900

The roots of Clovis lie in the treasured land of California. Yokut Indians, early inhabitants of the surrounding hills, made their livelihood from the natural bounty that existed here. Then, the Gold Rush of 1849 brought throngs of miners to California seeking to make their fortunes. The Gold Rush created a demand for beef to feed the miners and new settlers. The San Joaquin Valley was optimal grazing land. As early as 1870, cattlemen and sheepherders moved thousands of head through the wide valley and set up ranches. Others came to take advantage of the fertile land as a way to make their fortune through farming. Clovis Cole was among the early pioneers of the area to take such a risk. Moving here from the Midwest, Cole at one time had 40,000 acres all planted with wheat. Some saw land itself as a commodity. Large tracts of land were purchased by holding companies and marketed as developments called colonies, where buyers could own farms and build their homes. Advertisements enticing new settlers here appeared as far away as Europe. Cole lived with his family in the area that is now Old Town Clovis. Dirt roads crossed the region, and by the late 1800s, Front Street (now Clovis Avenue) was lined with wooden buildings selling wares. The budding community became a trading center for residents of the nearby agricultural colonies and foothills. In 1891, the town was given the name Clovis (Cole's first name) after Cole sold prime land to railroad developer Marcus Pollasky, with the condition that a train stop and a depot be built here. In 1892, local businessmen, including Cole, hired surveyor Inyroot Trilman to lay out a land map for the town's orderly growth. The community flourished to about 500 residents—complete with a schoolhouse, churches, and several saloons—and growth only continued when, in 1894, a 42-mile flume from the mountains moved fresh timber to a bustling lumber mill in Clovis that offered employment to many.

CLOVIS MARSHALL COLE. Born in 1856 in Indiana, Cole moved to a farm near present-day Clovis in the 1870s. His father, Stephen, gave him a team of four horses, and Cole made a business out of hauling lumber from the mountains. The entrepreneur used his earnings and began buying land in 1880, at a cost of $4 an acre, to farm wheat. By 1884, he had amassed 40,000 acres in Fresno and Madera Counties and had earned the title of "Wheat King." In 1891, Cole and his wife, Elizabeth, sold 480 acres of land for $4,000 in gold coin to railroad developer Marcus Pollasky. The railroad depot and town that grew around it were given Cole's first name, Clovis. Below is a rendering of Cole's residence. (Clovis Museum; Fresno County Public Library.)

EARLY MAP. This map depicts the budding village in 1891 that would become Clovis. The map shows the area that roughly covered one square mile of land that had been owned by Clovis Cole. It was bounded by Barstow, Sunnyside, Sierra, and Minnewawa Avenues. Today's Clovis Avenue was then called Front Street. Around the village, the vast land was dotted with cattle ranches, farms, and homesteads. (William T. Atkin.)

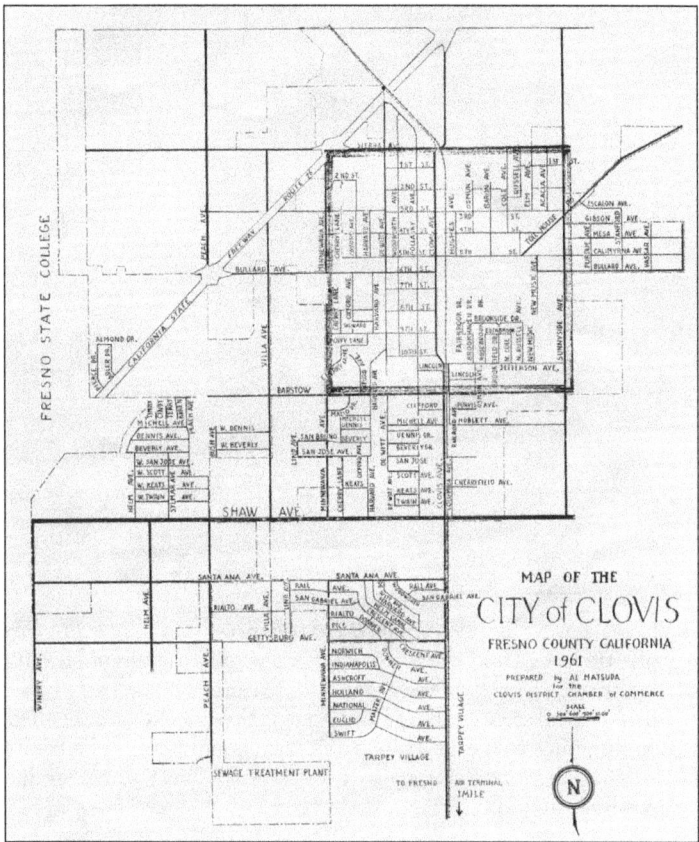

DRY FARMING. Due to limited rainfall and availability of irrigation, dry farming of wheat was widespread. Soil was loosely tilled so that when rain came, water could easily travel into the ground. It was tilled again after rain to prevent evaporation. Here, a mule team harvests wheat near Clovis in the late 1800s. (John Reynolds Collection.)

BUDDING TOWN. By 1893, shops lined the dirt roadway of Front Street (now Clovis Avenue) and became the social and economic hub of the growing town. Hitching posts for horses and shade-covered wooden porches were standard features on the early buildings. Robert E.L. Good built the first general store on Front and Fourth Streets (pictured) called R.E.L. Good's Cash Store. It was said to have sold everything from farm equipment and fabrics for clothing to dry goods and cooking supplies. There was also a drugstore, a livery stable, and, at one time, up to 10 saloons. (Clovis Museum; John Wright Collection.)

GETTING A DRINK. Will Jenkins sits atop a horse in front of the OK Saloon on Front Street, where beer is advertised on the wooden porch as costing 5¢ a glass in this undated photograph from the late 1800s. Pictured below, two unidentified men sit inside the saloon. According to a receipt from the Clovis establishment, proprietors Fraler and McKinsey provided "all standard brands of bottled goods" and "highest grades of wines, liquors and cigars."

GOODS AND WARES. The R.E.L. Good General Merchandise located on Front and Fourth Streets was rebuilt after the original store burned to the ground in the late 1800s. The buildings then were made primarily from timber. Many buildings were destroyed by fire during this time when, without an organized fire department, the community's only defense against flames was a volunteer bucket brigade. The interior of R.E.L. Good General Merchandise is pictured below with unnamed employees. The store was owned by Robert E.L. Good. His brothers were also Clovis merchants, with J.E. Good eventually opening a general merchandise store a block away from Robert Good's store. J.E. Good's mercantile had a community hall above his business.

BOUNTIFUL HARVEST. Pictured above, mule teams working the wheat fields converged by the livery stable in town. There, farmers and laborers could swap stories, pick up supplies, and discuss issues affecting the region. A growing topic of conversation involved moving crops and goods to expanding markets. Horse-drawn wagons (pictured) were a common means of transportation, but that would soon change with the growing prospects of a railroad coming to town. (Clovis Chamber of Commerce; John Reynolds Collection.)

MARCUS POLLASKY. Born in 1861 in Detroit, Pollasky earned a law degree, became president of a bank, and built a telegraph line from Chicago to Lake Superior. Health issues caused him to relocate in 1890 to California, where he promoted developing a railroad line that would bring Fresno County agriculture and timber products through the Sierra to Eastern markets. On February 23, 1891, Pollasky was elected president of the newly formed San Joaquin Valley Railroad. Using his natural charm, he worked tirelessly to acquire land, striking a deal with Clovis and Elizabeth Cole in December 1891. The to-be-constructed railroad depot and surrounding town would be named Clovis. Folklore says Clovis Cole's last name was not used because Cole Depot could have been confused with a coal depot. (Clovis Museum.)

FIRST TRACKS COMPLETED. The San Joaquin Valley Railroad received $1.6 million from San Francisco, Chicago, and New York banks, supporting the effort to build the 100-mile link through the mountain range. It was agreed that Marcus Pollasky would receive $100,000 if construction of the first 25 miles of track—from Fresno to Clovis to Hamptonville (Friant)—was finished within one year. Construction began with a festive ground-breaking on the Fourth of July, 1891. The track passed through Clovis in late 1891 and on January 20, 1892, reached to Hamptonville. Pollasky would receive his bonus. Southern Pacific Railroad provided flatcars and the locomotive to transport people along the new tracks to a grand celebration in Hamptonville. Pictured at the first shipment of wine by local train is Marcus Pollasky, seen standing between the drivers and wearing a tall hat. (Clovis Museum.)

BILL OF SALE. The document transferring ownership of land from Clovis and Elizabeth "Lizzie" Cole to Marcus Pollasky specifies the land is to be used for "railroad purposes" and that the buildings and fences on the land would remain the property of the Coles. The original document is located in the Clovis–Big Dry Creek Historical Society Museum today. (Clovis Museum.)

CLOVIS DEPOT. The railroad tracks were laid on the east of Front Street (Clovis Avenue). The depot was located at Fourth Street in a two-story wooden building with the same design that was used for the station built at Hamptonville (Friant)—temporarily named Pollasky—shown in this picture. As for continuing the tracks through the Sierra . . . that never occurred. In 1892, the San Joaquin Valley Railroad Company faltered financially, Pollasky returned to the East, and the tracks that had been placed to Hamptonville (Friant) were auctioned on the Fresno County court house steps to Southern Pacific Railroad. Folklore says many locals thought Pollasky a swindler who disappeared with the invested money. Hamptonville stripped Pollasky's name from the town. A street in Clovis, however, remains named in Pollasky's honor. The railroad did boost the vibrancy of the young town. A century later, the tracks would be removed and replaced with the Old Town Clovis Trail. (Clovis Museum.)

COLONY SYSTEM. Much of the area surrounding the village of Clovis was populated and developed through the system of agricultural colonies. Around 1860, much of the San Joaquin Valley was classified as "swamplands" when Henry Miller claimed to travel the region by boat—a boat that he later confessed was strapped to his wagon. Nevertheless, the classification made the rich valley farmland available for a cheap price, and Miller and other land speculators including William Chapman purchased large holdings. Chapman, the largest landholder in California, owning nearly a million acres in 1871, was instrumental in creating the Central California Colony based on the ideas of Bernard Marks. The plan called for securing water rights for a large tract of land and breaking the land into 20-acre parcels to be sold to farmers. The buyers were required to irrigate the land, plant their crops, and build their homes. Pictured is Clovis Cole's Red Bank Ranch. (Fresno County Public Library.)

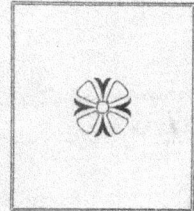

MARKETING APPEAL. The Central California Colony, located southwest of Fresno, was successful in bringing settlers to the Central Valley. Affordable land and irrigation were made available to those willing to work hard and start a new life in a region previously ignored by pioneers. Around Clovis, colonies such as Garfield, Red Banks, Scandinavian, and Temperance emerged. Advertisements marketing the opportunity to become a landowner were placed in local newspapers (pictured) as well as in East Coast and even European publications. Some colonies sought out like-minded residents. Temperance Colony was a religious group that did not allow drinking, and Scandinavian Colony was made up of people of Scandinavian descent. (Clovis Chamber of Commerce.)

SCHOOLHOUSES. The colony system united its inhabitants as neighbors and as a community. Schoolhouses were constructed to provide a place where the children of the settlement and surrounding area could be educated. Jefferson School, pictured above, was established in 1884. The land for the school, located at present-day Shaw and Fowler Avenues, was donated by the Cole family. Below, Garfield School, established in 1883, provided a place for students from the Garfield Colony, which was named after Pres. James A. Garfield. The original wooden schoolhouse was located at Shepherd and Minnewawa Avenues and was later rebuilt using a brick facade. A fire in 1990 gutted the building, but the brick archway remains intact at that location today. Garfield Elementary School is now located at Peach and Nees Avenues. (Fresno County Public Library.)

COLONY LIFESTYLE. It was not uncommon for men of a settlement to join together in some of life's routine chores. In the undated photograph above, six men pause before heading out on a hunting party. Below, land is plowed on a farm. Crops included grain, grapes, and tree fruit. (Ingmire-Bradley family; John Reynolds Collection.)

MOUNTAIN CROP. Growth in the region spurred another prosperous industry: lumber. In 1894, after four years of construction, the Fresno Flume and Irrigation Co. completed a 42-mile flume that connected the wooded region near Shaver to a lumberyard in Clovis on the east side of Front Street just south of Fifth Street. The flume carried cut lumber to Clovis—as much as 200,000 board feet per day—and provided pitch-laden irrigation water. Water from the flume was piped under Front Street and down Bullard Avenue, ending around Willow Avenue. Some homeowners used this water. (Clovis Unified School District; Clovis Chamber of Commerce.)

C. B. SHAVER, President   FIRST NATIONAL BANK, Treasurer
A. B. LONG, Vice President   C. W. MUSICK, Secretary

Fresno Flume and
Irrigation Company

Incorporated October 31, 1891
Capital Stock, $500,000

Manufacturers of and Dealers in SUGAR PINE, WHITE PINE and FIR LUMBER
Also BOXES, TRAYS, SHAKES and ALL KINDS OF
BUILDING MATERIAL

◆◆◆◆

Timbers in Extra Sizes and Lengths a Specialty

Thirty Million Feet of Lumber Shipped This Year.
One Thousand Employes Wish Every Reader Good Cheer.

Mills at Shaver
Box Factory and Planing Mill at Clovis

Fresno Office
Fresno National Bank Building

TELEPHONE 177

General Office at Clovis
J. G. FERGUSON
Financier

DETERMINED PATH. The flume began under the present site of Shaver Dam at 5,275 feet above sea level and descended 4,900 feet over 42 miles. The V-shaped trough was built of wood secured tight enough to hold running water and carry loose boards. It was supported by stacked trestles as high as 90 feet and made of units called boxes that were 16 feet long; 330 boxes made one mile. Twelve flume-tender houses connected by a single telephone wire were spaced along the flume's route. The tenders could alert one another to trouble along the waterway, and a catwalk on the side of the flume let men patrol the flume between stations. Occasionally, a passenger missing the stagecoach from Shaver would ride a flume boat down the mountain. (Fresno County Public Library.)

TOLLHOUSE ROAD. While rough wood was sent down the waterways of the flume to the mill in Clovis, wagons pulled by horses, mules, or oxen carried prime lumber to the yard by way of Tollhouse Road, constructed for this specific purpose. The perilous, steep grade was made available to the public but required a toll fee of $1.50 for a wagon and a span of horses; an additional span of horses was 50¢; a horse and buggy, $1; horseman, 50¢; pack or lead animal, 25¢; loose horses, mules or cattle, 10¢ a head; and sheep and hogs, 2¢ each. (Clovis Chamber of Commerce.)

LUMBERYARD. The Fresno Flume and Irrigation Co. yard in Clovis had a small pond that received lumber from the flume. The 40-acre site included a box factory, planing mill, and processing areas that were powered by a large steam plant and kilns. Billowing out of the smokestacks was foul-smelling smoke, which was made worse by mixing with rotting bark. Generally, the odor stayed downwind from town. (John Reynolds Collection.)

MILL EMPLOYMENT. Clovis mill workers at the Fresno Flume and Irrigation Co. on Front Street pose in this undated photograph. At the beginning of its operation, the mill employed 140 men and had a yearly payroll of $450,000. By the company's second year of operation, it had between 300 and 500 workers on the payroll. (Clovis Chamber of Commerce.)

GROWING TOWN. This late-1890s image, taken from the Fresno Flume and Irrigation Co. lumberyard that was located only a few blocks southeast of Clovis, shows the development of the young community. The businesses seen here face onto the dirt road of Front Street. Across the way, the railroad tracks and depot can be seen. (John Wright Collection.)

FARMERS MARKET. Produce from outlying farms would be brought into town to be sold each week. This photograph from the late 1800s shows fresh melons available. At this time, there was not a butcher shop in town. Periodically meat was brought in from a Madera butcher and sold to Clovis residents. (Ingmire-Bradley family.)

1678- Grammar School. Clovis, California

GRAMMAR SCHOOL. Clovis children had to be sent out of town for schooling, but by 1895 the population of the young community had grown to support its own school. That March, citizens requested from the county superintendent that a Clovis Board of Trustees be established. Appointed were Clovis Cole, H.A. Koulke, and J.A. Ferguson. At the board's first meeting on March 27, 1895, the top item of business was building a schoolhouse. The board pursued a $5,000 bond to fund it, and the community approved it on August 10 by a vote of 25-0. School began September 19, 1895. Students met at Southern Pacific Railroad's warehouse until construction of the school at Pollasky and Second Streets was completed in 1897. Pictured are the grammar school and a group of students in the late 1800s. (Fresno County Public Library; Clovis Chamber of Commerce.)

CLOVIS MILL FIRE. Fire ravaged the Fresno Flume and Irrigation Co. lumberyard in 1898. Workers could only stand and watch as there was little defense against the flames that engulfed the stacks of wood and sawdust shavings. The factory, warehouse, planing mill, and engine house all burned to the ground, but they were soon rebuilt and the company continued to prosper. (Clovis Chamber of Commerce.)

Two

TURN OF THE 20TH CENTURY
1900 TO 1911

As the city grew into the 20th century, the population surrounding the town center approached 500 citizens. Homes were springing up around the business core. The prime location was north and west of the mill, to avoid the stench spewing from the smokestacks on the mill property and carried on by the prevailing winds from the northwest. Businesses expanded along Front Street and Pollasky Avenue. As fires destroyed some of the original wooden structures, they were replaced with more substantial brick and mortar buildings, showing a commitment to Clovis as a lasting community. Several saloons lined the main street. Hotels were built to accommodate mill workers and visitors to the area. Livery stables thrived on business from the lumberyard and local drayage requirements of colony farmers. In 1904, the community members celebrated the opening of the First State Bank, where residents could earn interest on deposits and those needing loans to purchase land could obtain needed funds. Two newspapers were started. One was short-lived, and the other eventually merged with another and reported to the community for more than 100 years. The Southern Pacific Railroad continued to transport goods and travelers through the town and adjacent valley communities. Churches were built and congregations worshipped together as well as gave service in the community. People from various backgrounds established their new home in Clovis and brought a rich cultural heritage to the California valley town. Clovis was becoming more than just a stop on the railroad line and a site for lumber processing. As growth continued, it was evident that basic community services were needed and desired, including a water system, sewer system, organized firefighting, and law enforcement. The incorporation of Clovis as an independent city was proposed to provide the structure that would give these services to the growing town.

EVERYDAY LIFE. Mrs. Russell, right, readies boiling water in preparation for doing laundry. Wash day for a home was a laborious project during the early 1900s, with large tubs being used in the yard for hand scrubbing the wash with a wooden agitator. It took two people to wring out the heavy garments and hang them to dry. (Ingmire-Bradley family.)

SOCIAL LIFE. Work filled most days, but there was still time to be social. Under the shade of the trees, to escape the summer heat, families would sometimes gather to visit and celebrate. Clovis had song festivals, baseball games, dances, church activities, picnics, debates, and spelling bees. At Christmastime, people in the colonies and town would practice for weeks to present a special musical program. (Clovis Museum.)

HOMES IN CLOVIS. Pictured above is the Ingmire Home, originally built on the west side of Pollasky Avenue between Third and Fourth Streets (now located at Seventh and Pollasky Streets). The first homes were built of wooden boards, gaps overlapped with narrower strips and very little interior support. By 1910, when this house was constructed, tall and narrow windows, finials, and fish-scale shingles adorned the most luxurious homes. (Ingmire-Bradley family.)

FRONT STREET. This 1909 photograph of Front Street looks south from Fourth Street. Robert E.L. Good's mercantile is on the near corner. Southward is the Clovis Bar and the OK Saloon, as well as several other saloons. On the far corner is J.E. Good's General Merchandise. Streets were generally dusty in summer and muddy in the winter. (Clovis Museum.)

LIVERY STABLE. The town livery stable rented out horses and buggies, much as car rental agencies provide vehicles today. Originally, two livery stables operated in Clovis, Ingmire Brothers (pictured), and Turner's. After hauling loads, drivers and muleskinners would spend time between jobs pitching horseshoes and exchanging the latest news at the stables. At one time, Ingmire's was where folks would pick up their mail. (Ingmire-Bradley family.)

HIGH SCHOOL. Children attending school past eighth grade had to travel out of town. In 1899, Jefferson Colony farmer Lee Beall and mill worker John Rutledge organized seven school districts (Red Banks, Jefferson, Garfield, Mississippi, Wolters Colony, Temperance, and Clovis) to form Clovis Union High School. Students met at Clovis Grammar School until 1902, when the high school was built at Fifth and Osmun Avenues. (John Wright Collection.)

BUSINESS EXPANSION. When L.W. Gibson's General Merchandise wooden store burned, replacing it at Fourth and Pollasky Avenues was a more expansive brick store that offered a wider variety of merchandise. Pictured in 1906, from left to right, are Mr. Kerr, Pearl Drury (later known as Mrs. Harry Ball), Bert Herwell, L.W. Gibson, Clyde Gibson, Harry Atkinson, Arthur Ruby, and Floyd Redford. (Clovis Unified School District.)

COPPER MINE. Five miles north of Clovis near Copper Avenue, Fresno Copper Company mined deep into the ground. Many miners were Clovis people, and Clovis was the nearest town where workers would shop or socialize on a Saturday night. This 1906 picture shows the mining operation that, at times, had 50 men on the payroll. The mine eventually played out and by 1920 was dismantled. (Fresno County Public Library.)

ESTABLISHING HOUSES OF WORSHIP. In the early days, people would travel from the surrounding area to worship at open-air meetings. Later, as congregations grew, meetings were held in gathering halls or rooms rented from local businesses. In 1909, members of the Catholic church rented Robert E. Good's Hall for $2 and celebrated the first Mass in Clovis with about 40 worshippers in attendance. A Methodist church was constructed in 1893 near the downtown. In 1903, the First Baptist Church (pictured above) was constructed on Fourth and DeWitt Streets. The First Presbyterian Church was established in 1898 on Woodworth Avenue with a permanent building, pictured below, constructed in 1903. (John Reynolds Collection.)

FIFTH STREET, LOOKING EAST, CLOVIS, CAL.

PREDICTION COMING TRUE. On June 15, 1894, the headline in the *Fresno Weekly Republican* read "A Hamlet That Will Soon Become a Big Town." The article about Clovis said, "The bringing down of the big flume of the Fresno Flume and Irrigation Company as far as Clovis, only eight miles from Fresno, must cause many regrets that the flume was not completed to Fresno. Nevertheless there is wide spread satisfaction at the brilliant future which certainly awaits the village of Clovis." Shortly after 1900, windmills were installed at the more affluent residences to provide running water. Telephone lines, seen in these photographs, were a sign of progress. (The first telephone was installed at R.E.L. Good's establishment.) Above is Fifth Street looking east toward the mill and the elevated flume. Below is Pollasky Avenue around 1910. (John Reynolds Collection.)

4TH. ST. AT. POLLASKY AVE, CLOVIS CAL.

TALL ORDER. Pictured above, stacks of rough-cut lumber reach heights of up to 30 feet. Lumber that traveled the waterway of the V-shaped flume from the Shaver area would drop into a pond on the mill grounds on Front Street south of Fifth Street. The lumber would have to be stacked to dry and to be stored. Many of the orders at the mill were for agricultural crates that area farmers used to transport produce. The Fresno Flume and Irrigation Co. could move 200,000 board feet during a day. Below, this undated photograph shows employees of the mill. In the early 1900s, general labor employees received $1.35 per day. Luther E. Weldon, the company engineer, earned $2. (Stan King.)

HOBLITT HOTEL. Built by Joshua Carmen Hoblitt in 1902 at Fourth Street and Pollasky Avenue, the Hoblitt Hotel provided refined lodging. Popular with traveling men, schoolteachers, and visiting businessmen, the three-story building had a small parlor and rooms for rent. The top floor burned in 1927. The lower floors were reconstructed and remain today. A restaurant now occupies the lower floor with offices on the second floor. (John Reynolds Collection.)

WORKING MAN'S RESIDENCE. With 400 workers at the lumber company, there was a need for lodging. The company built a boardinghouse near the mill. The B.K. Smith Hotel, pictured in 1910 on Front Street, provided rooms, as did the Byron Hotel just down the road. The back porch of the Smith hotel had a wash bench, sink, and soap so the men could clean up.

SOUTHERN PACIFIC RAILROAD. The rails laid by Marcus Pollasky's San Joaquin Valley Railroad investors in 1891 and later purchased by Southern Pacific Railroad provided a comfortable, reliable form of transportation for those traveling in a passenger car, such as the one pictured above in 1910. The tracks that connected trains from the main line up to Clovis were also used to move lumber and freight to market. In 1911, grape growing and packing were becoming an important agricultural sector, and a raisin-processing plant was built just north of the Clovis Depot. Trains stopped in Melvin (Jefferson and Clovis Avenues) and Glorietta (Herndon near Minnewawa Avenues) to service the packing sheds that were built along the rail line. Below, workers from Stewart Packing House (Clovis and Shaw Avenues) are pictured in 1913. (John Reynolds Collection.)

FIRST CLOVIS NEWSPAPERS. "A Clean Paper for Clean People," the *Clovis Tribune* heralded. It made its debut in March 1905 and was published Fridays with a one-year subscription of $1.50. In 1911, H.W. McCormick, believed to be the paper's founder, sold the paper to H.E. Armstrong, who remained as editor for 25 years in the office located on Pollasky Avenue (seen seated at right below in 1911). The early editions of the *Clovis Tribune* were like community newsletters, announcing weddings, deaths, and visits from out-of-town guests, as well as descriptions of new merchandise in local shops. In 1910, the *Clovis Observer*, a four-page tabloid, was published briefly by E.M. Harwell. The *Clovis Tribune* remained the only paper in town until 1918, when S.S. Case and his wife, May, moved to Clovis and began publishing the *Clovis Independent*. The *Tribune* and *Independent* would eventually merge in 1942. (Clovis Chamber of Commerce; Clovis Museum.)

Three

INCORPORATION
1912

The 20 years of growth that followed the opening of the railroad, flume, and lumber mill in Clovis yielded a vibrant, prosperous town. Clovis was now home to many families, farms, schools, and businesses. The town had no organized government but did have some services provided by Fresno County, such as a constable and justice of the peace. As the years passed, the community of roughly 500 had an identity of its own and citizens began working toward establishing a government of their own as well. By the end of 1911, the talk of the town was incorporating Clovis as a full-fledged city. Voters approved incorporating the one square mile bounded by Minnewawa, Barstow, Sunnyside, and Sierra Avenues. It became the City of Clovis on February 27, 1912. The vote was 169 in favor and 83 against. The members of the board of trustees, which operated like the city council, were Lewis W. Gibson, who was named president (mayor), Robert E.L. Good, Richard Norrish, A.E.D. Scott, and Frank Drury. Two months later in April, an election for trustees was again held and developed into a battle over whether Clovis would be a dry town. The dry panel won. Notes from the first meeting on April 27, 1912, show that the new board wasted no time in taking action to rid the community of alcohol. "J.C. Harchman (Horschman) was elected City Marshall and the first reading of Police regulations was read, relating to and making it unlawful the keeping of places where intoxicating liquors are sold. Carried unanimously." That first year, the board usually met at R.E.L. Good's store, since there was no city hall. Items decided included matters about taxes, creation of a fire district, and regulations about new construction. One of the more important decisions occurred in August when the board called for election of a bond to pay for building a city sewer system for $24,000 and water system for $25,000. Voters overwhelmingly passed the bond, and construction began later that year. With that, the foundations for a modern city were laid.

CITY OF CLOVIS. Pictured in 1912, J.E. Good General Merchandise anchored the northwest corner of Front and Fifth Streets. The town was well established with commerce, industry, homes, churches, and schools, and officially became a city on February 27, 1912. The city had become a trade center for farmers and lumbermen living around it. Incorporation meant local tax dollars and funds for community projects. Streets, streetlights, alleys, health and sanitation, and fire control were all on that year's agenda. Some of the bigger problems of the time were the streets south of Fifth Street where sloughs ran through, especially on Ninth and Tenth Streets. Sometimes, those streets, which were leveled from swampland, were impassible, and occasionally a wagon could be seen stuck in the mud in the middle of the road. (Monte Head.)

BEFORE THE BOARD OF SUPERVISORS OF THE COUNTY OF FRESNO,

STATE OF CALIFORNIA.

* *

IN THE MATTER OF CANVASSING THE   *
RETURNS OF THE ELECTION ON THE   *
PROPOSITION TO INCORPORATE THE   *
CITY OF CLOVIS AND FOR MUNICIPAL   *
OFFICERS OF SAID CITY.   *

    *

    *

    *

         Pursuant to law, the Board of Supervisors of the County of Fresno met on Monday, February 19th, 1912, as the Board of Canvassers to canvass the votes polled at Clovis in the County of Fresno, State of California, at an election held on the 15th day of February, 1912, for the purpose of determining whether a certain portion of the County of Fresno should be incorporated under the name of "City of Clovis",--

         And it appearing from the affidavit of W. H. Sowell filed herein that the order and notice of said election heretofore made by this Board was published in The Clovis Tribune, a newspaper printed and published within the boundaries of said proposed corporation for two weeks next preceding said election ,--

         And the returns from the Precinct at which such election was held having been received, the board now proceeds to open and canvass said votes and does find from said returns that said vote is as follows, to wit:-

         There were cast "For Incorporation"   _169_ votes.

         There were cast "Against Incorporation"   _83_ votes.

PEACEFUL TOWN. Prior to incorporation, Clovis had little government except for that provided by Fresno County. There was a jail near the Clovis Depot, and a county constable or justice of the peace could be summoned. Clovis was relatively peaceful, and guns were not commonly carried. The city's safety grew when Jake C. Horschman was appointed city marshall in February 1912. One of the first city ordinances set up rules for operating saloons and imposed a tax of $100 per saloon. By April, the town voted to be rid of saloons altogether. (State of California.)

OFFICERS OF THE CITY. Pictured in April 1912 are, from left to right (seated) Perry R. Jackson, trustee; Lewis W. Gibson, president; A.E.D. Schott, trustee; and John Shackelford, trustee; (standing) Albert S. Kirkpatrick, city recorder; Jake C. Horschman, city marshall; Dr. J.S. Boynton, trustee; L.E. Weldon, city clerk; and Floyd W. Redford, city treasurer; When Clovis was incorporated in February, a board of trustees was established, and an election for a new board was held in April. The election turned into a battle over liquor, and the dry panel candidates won. According to minutes from one of the first board meetings, "places where intoxicating liquors are sold" were immediately made unlawful. (Clovis Museum.)

GIBSON HOUSE. This home at 940 Third Street was built by Lewis W. Gibson when he was the first mayor of Clovis in 1912. The architect is unknown, but local tradesmen built the 2,700-square-foot residence that includes beamed ceilings, a built-in china hutch, and plate shelves. The residence—including the original carriage house—remains intact today, and it now includes the addition of a bathroom in the 1960s and a garage in the 1970s. City founder Clovis Cole's family residence was located not too far away, on the east side of Osmun Street just north of Third Street. Cole later moved to a home at 304 Harvard Avenue, near Third Street, that also remains standing today. (Clovis Museum.)

Four

FOUNDATIONS OF
THE NEW CITY
1913 TO 1930

Clovis settled into a way of life following the incorporation of the city. Lasting structure and order were added to the town. Local citizens shared their input and support as the Clovis Board of Trustees (predecessors to the Clovis City Council) took steps to develop municipal services.

Townsfolk benefitted from water and sewer systems, paved streets and streetlights, and organized law enforcement and fire protection. Telephone poles dotted the sides of the road, and automobiles began to replace the horse and buggy. Social life picked up as families from the outlying colonies and nearby foothill communities came to Clovis for dances at McCord's Hall. There were music recitals, poetry readings, and plays. Service clubs emerged, and key among them was the Clovis Women's Club. The club held a fundraiser in the spring of 1914 that featured food and games. Ranchers and farmers made a temporary arena by circling their wagons around a vacant lot, and folks competed in mule riding and calf roping. The festival became an annual event that would evolve into the Clovis Rodeo. The city also experienced hardships. National events influenced the town. World War I brought a rise in patriotism as the community mourned the loss of Cecil Cox, the first hometown soldier killed in action. The American Legion Cecil Cox Post 147, named in his honor, formed in 1919 to support the military. The effects of what would become the Great Depression were already being felt in Clovis in the mid-1920s. Falling crop prices and the closure of the mill left many struggling financially. The October 15, 1925, *Clovis Tribune* reported there were more unoccupied houses in Clovis than at any time in its history (62 vacant houses and 10 vacant businesses). "The dull times have driven many to other points to get employment," the article stated. The population of Clovis actually dropped from 1920 to 1930 by about 200, with 1,314 people calling Clovis home. A feisty town from the start, Clovis would bounce back.

CLOVIS MELTING POT. American immigration around 1900 was among the largest in history. People came from Italy, China, Japan, Armenia, Mexico, India, and other countries to start new lives. They became vintners, farmers, businessmen, stonecutters, railroad workers, laundry operators, restaurant owners, laborers in orchards and vineyards, and mill workers. Clovis became a town of many blended cultures. (Clovis Chamber of Commerce.)

NEW HOME. As a young woman in Italy, Ismene Grossi began exchanging letters with Siro Grossi, a handsome stonecutter living at her sister's Vermont boardinghouse. Eventually, he wrote to ask Ismene to marry him. He paid her passage but said that if she chose not to marry him, he would pay for her return trip. The two wed and, in 1924, set up their home in Clovis. (Grossi family.)

PROVIDING PUBLIC WATER. Providing citizens with a clean, dependable water source was a high priority for the new board of trustees. Shortly after their election, a site at Fifth Street near the railroad tracks was selected and the water tower built. According to Arthur Chedister, who observed the building of the tower, "The well at the present site was drilled during the summer of 1913. In the fall construction of the present high steel tank was started. The rivets in the entire structure were hand driven and it was a thrilling sight to watch the iron workers put up the tank. They were suspended in the air, it seemed, swinging sledgehammers, driving home the red hot rivets. When they tested the tank, there was not a single leak in the whole tank. When the tank was completed, practically every boy in high school, except for a few 'sissies,' climbed to the top of the tank and back before authorities finally stopped it." The tower holds 60,000 gallons. (Ingmire-Bradley family.)

EARLY VOLUNTEER FIRE DEPARTMENT. Fire was a constant threat to the wooden buildings of early Clovis. When fire broke out, the whistle would sound at the Fresno Flume and Irrigation Company, sending volunteers, primarily from the mill, running to fight the blaze. In 1912, construction of the first Clovis firehouse was authorized. In 1913, an alarm system (left) was a bell at the top of a tower in downtown Clovis; it was constructed for $122 in donations from merchants. In July 1913, the fire company was authorized to purchase the four coats and helmets pictured on four of the eight men standing on the tower. In 1916, the city passed an ordinance officially creating the Clovis Volunteer Fire Department. Pictured below is the department's first motorized fire truck, purchased in 1916 at a cost of $1,175.

Polasky Ave North. Clovis Calif.

ELECTRIC STREETLIGHT. While electric streetlights were used in America as early as 1880, much of the western United States did not make the change until well into the 20th century. During its early years, Clovis used kerosene lamps to illuminate the downtown area, which proved to be a dangerous fire hazard on many occasions. But with the increase in automobiles and evening pedestrian traffic in the 1910s, Clovis made the change to electric streetlights. The large lamps were suspended over the street by electrical wires, as seen in this undated photograph of Pollasky Avenue. (John Reynolds Collection.)

KEEPING ORDER, BATTLING BOOTLEGGING. Charles Clifford (pictured), the town constable from 1896 to 1924, worked with town marshall J.C. Horschman in keeping Clovis safe. Crime was generally low, but the officers did find themselves battling bootlegging following the city's move in 1912 to make alcohol illegal. Those wanting a drink were clever. According to the memoirs of local Arthur Chedister, around 1914 a large barrel of whiskey was shipped to the Clovis Depot addressed to "John Doe." Clifford and Horschman rolled the barrel out on the platform and left it in plain sight. The officers then hid, taking turns watching the barrel in order to nab whoever claimed it. After three days of the stakeout, the barrel remained untouched. That day, though, the depot agent accidentally bumped the large barrel while moving freight. To his surprise, it rolled easily. The barrel was empty. Clifford popped out of his hiding spot and discovered someone had gone under the platform, bored a hole through the platform and barrel, and drained the whiskey away, presumably in several buckets. (Clovis Museum.)

54

SMOOTH RIDE. With the release of the Ford Model T in 1908, automobiles began to arrive on the scene in Clovis in the 1910s. For a time, the dirt roads sufficed. But cars became more abundant and began to replace the horse and carriage as the primary means of transportation. By the 1920s, citizens voted to support a bond to pay for construction of paved streets. These 1922 photographs provided by Gail William Forbes show workers grading and paving the new streets of Pollasky and Clovis Avenues. Harvey Rinehart, the grandfather of Gail William Forbes, was superintendent of the project. Her uncle Gail Reinhart was the timekeeper. (Gail William Forbes.)

CITY STAFF GROWS. Slowly, city departments emerged and workers were hired to care for the operations of the town. Pictured in this late-1920s photograph are two employees of the city's Street and Water Department. Municipal services began in some form early on. It was the Clovis Women's Club, a group of active women who sought out projects for the good of the community, which first approached the city's town council in 1913 seeking to establish a cleanup day when a wagon would make the rounds and pick up rubbish. (John Wright Collection.)

IRRIGATION YIELDS ABUNDANT CROPS. Early farmers found the fertile San Joaquin Valley soil would yield an abundant variety of crops with irrigation. In some areas, rough ditches tapped into the river waters. Later, canals were built to optimize irrigation. The Enterprise Canal and Irrigation Company was administered by Joseph D. Reyburn, J.P. Vincent, Joseph Chance, Jacob Cole, and Steven Hamilton. The Enterprise Canal, first started in the late 1880s at the Kings River near the foothills, was completed as far as Garfield Colony in 1890. The canal company was organized and financed by the land owners benefitting from the irrigation water. Pictured above is a wagon load of watermelons bound for market about 1900. Below is a picture postcard of the Monte Cassino Wine Company that operated in Clovis during the 1910s. (John Reynolds Collection.)

VINEYARDS AND WINERIES
MONTE CASSINO WINE CO., CLOVIS, CALIFORNIA

BANKING IN CLOVIS. Proprietor Robert E.L. Good acted as a banker from his store, providing loans to farmers. He and a group of citizens would later organize a bank called First State Bank of Clovis in 1903. It operated from a building in back of Good's store, which was replaced with a brick building (that later was used as the post office). In 1912, the bank constructed a building on the corner of Fourth and Pollasky Streets (pictured) with grand pillars and stairs that looked very impressive to townsfolk. The bank prospered for several years, reaching deposits of $1.5 million, but falling crop prices in the 1920s put several bank loans into trouble. The bank was on the brink of closure when Pres. Franklin Delano Roosevelt closed all banks and set up government insurance for all deposits. First State Bank of Clovis did not reopen, and the building was then used as the Justice Court. Today, the building houses the Clovis–Big Dry Creek Historical Society Museum and still contains the bank's original vault. (Clovis Unified School District.)

OWL AND LONE WOLF. The First State Bank of Clovis was robbed at gunpoint on February 5, 1924. Thomas "The Owl" Griffin and his accomplice, Felix "The Lone Wolf" Sloper parked their stolen Chandler outside of the bank and entered the building around 1:00 p.m. Assistant cashier Tommy Howison was the only one inside. Griffin approached Howison at the enclosed cashier window, pictured, and asked him to break a $20 bill. Sloper meanwhile snuck to the back door and into the area where Howison stood. "The next thing I knew, I was looking down the wrong end of a gun," Howison recalled. The cashier was tied up and locked in the walk-in vault. The robbers stole the contents of the safe and tills and were about to leave when bank vice president Emory Reyburn arrived. The robbers pushed him against a far wall and fled to the car, still running outside. As they drove away, they threw handfuls of nails onto the street and tossed the gun in a muddy field near Tarpey. They were later captured. (Clovis Museum.)

FIFTH
ANNUAL FESTIVAL
OF CLOVIS
SATURDAY, APRIL 24, 1920

Under Auspices of the

Woman's Club and American Legion

Grand Parade At 10 o'Clock

BASKET DINNER IN THE PARK

Horse Racing and Rodeo		Airplane Flights
All Kinds of Foot Racing	Big Carnival Attractions	Various Other Amusements
$1 Cash in Prize For Best Showing In the Parade	Dancing Afternoon and Evening	$5 Cash Prize Winner $5 Horse Race

Entertainment in the Evening at the Auditorium

Happy Jack and His Broncho Busters Have Charge of the Rodeo

HANDSOME PRIZE TO WINNER OF BUCKING CONTEST

CLOVIS WOMEN'S CLUB. In 1912, a group of 15 ladies organized the Clovis Women's Club, which was devoted to promoting social, educational, and civic improvements. The club founded a park at First and Front (Clovis) Streets, organized the city's first community cleanup day, and helped raise money for a hospital. The Women's Club is likely best known for starting what would become the Clovis Rodeo and Clovis Rodeo Parade. In the spring of 1914, the group held a fundraiser. Wagons and a few automobiles ringed a vacant lot on Fourth and Pollasky Streets to form a corral for mule riding and calf roping. The festival also included booths, games, and races. The festival (parade) queen was Marion D. Armstrong, whose mother was president of the club and whose father published the *Clovis Tribune*. The festival raised $700, and became an annual event. Pictured above, children ride atop Garfield School's float. At left, a 1920 advertisement in the *Clovis Tribune* touts the festival. (Clovis Museum; Clovis Tribune.)

CLOVIS RODEO. Local cowboys and ranchers looked forward to the annual Clovis Festival and Horse Show and having the chance to show off their roping and riding skills. As interest grew, more horses and cattle appeared and a rodeo competition was set up. The event evolved to become the Clovis Rodeo, which is still held annually the last weekend of April. The enthusiasm for the event was evident from its start. The *Clovis Tribune* reported in 1916 that all stores closed the afternoon of the festival and that 1,000 pounds of beef were donated, barbecued, and given for free to those attending. A band played, a "beautiful baby" contest was held, and local military units presented a drill and march. Mayor Lewis Gibson tried to give a speech but was "sentenced" to eat three hot dogs. (Nick Ubick.)

ENGINEERING MARVEL REDUCED TO SCRAP. During the winter of 1914, snowstorms wrecked part of the 42-mile wooden flume that ran from Shaver in the Sierra Nevada to the lumber mill in Clovis. World War I began before the flume was repaired, and the attempt to repair the flume was abandoned. About 1920, the flume was sold to the Independent Lumber Company, which dismantled the flume and sold the lumber for scrap. The *Clovis Tribune* carried this advertisement to "buy cheap lumber." The dismantling operation took over a year to complete. For a while, trucks were used to transport lumber from the mountains to the Clovis mill, but the mill closed in 1925. As a vital part of the Clovis economy for several decades, its ruin was greatly felt in the community. (Clovis Tribune.)

52. Clovis Union High School, Clovis Calif.

"MODERN, UP-TO-DATE" CLOVIS HIGH SCHOOL. The original Clovis Union High School built in 1902 was demolished, and the "Mediterranean-style" new school was built on the same location with funds from a $100,000 school bond passed in 1919. The structure was designed by prominent California architect William Weeks. His designs for public buildings, private homes, and even a bridge earned him contracts for 22 Carnegie libraries between 1902 and 1921. A *Clovis Tribune* article dated September 30, 1920, listed courses at the new school including drawing, history, physical training for girls, music, domestic science, language, English, manual training, and science and mathematics. Today, the building houses San Joaquin College of Law. Pictured below is an early Clovis High baseball team. Baseball was popular in early Clovis, setting the stage for future excellence in athletics. (John Reynolds Collection; Clovis Museum.)

Clovis Apr 24 1904

LANDMARK HOTEL FOR SALE. America was recovering from World War I and was back on the road to prosperity. Businesses were beginning to boom in many areas. However, the well-established and prominent Hoblitt Hotel on Pollasky Avenue in Clovis apparently was not. In the August 1920 edition of the *Clovis Tribune* appeared this advertisement touting the grand amenities of 32 rooms with hot and cold water, electric lights, and "A Splendid Opportunity for a Live, Hustling Hotel Man." After it was sold by Fanny Guptill Hoblitt to W.M. Foster, the building's name changed to the Hotel Lillie Frances in honor of Foster's two daughters. (Clovis Tribune.)

FIRE DAMAGES HOTEL. In 1927, fire broke out on the third floor of the Lillie Frances Hotel, formerly the Hoblitt Hotel. As the alarm bell sounded, student Nick Ubick was at the nearby Clovis High School. Enrolled in a photography class, he grabbed his camera and headed for the hotel fire. He snapped these pictures of the fire and returned to school. In the 1970s, his son found unprinted negatives at the Ubick home and had them printed. These are the images that emerged. The hotel was reconstructed without the third story. Ownership changed hands several times over the next 20 years. In 1942–1943, it was a hospital with attending physician Dr. Wilbur Lose. His office remained in the building until 1955. (Nick Ubick.)

FALLEN SOLDIER. John Cecil Cox, born in 1897, became the first casualty of World War I from Clovis when he was killed in action in 1918. The community mourned the loss, and in 1919 the American Legion Cecil Cox Post 147 was established in Clovis and named in his honor. The Legion remains active today with more than 600 members. (Clovis Museum.)

Five

CHALLENGING TIMES
1930 TO 1960

The years between 1930 and 1960 were characterized by both great struggles and great achievements. The lives of Clovis citizens became intertwined as the challenges of those years brought opportunities for building a stronger community. Clovis citizens felt the lasting effects of the Great Depression in 1929. Money was tight, businesses failed, and families struggled to make ends meet. The Dust Bowl, which began in 1930, drove people from their Great Plains homes. Many moved to the San Joaquin Valley hoping for employment, but conditions were not much better in Clovis. A center of the grape-growing industry, Fresno County suffered dire hardship that would take years and a concerted effort by determined farmers to overcome. World War II broke out, encompassing the globe and touching the lives of Clovis citizens. Japanese Americans were relocated, local high school graduates postponed their educations to enlist in the armed services, and lives given in the service of country were honored in 1949 with a new community building. At the same time, a battle of another kind was being waged. The polio epidemic that began in 1916 was still a threat until 1960. The town was fortunate to have several dedicated medical professionals attending to the needs of community members. As challenges arose, there were great demonstrations of friendship. Friends looked after friends' farms in their absence. Families watched out for one another, often lending a hand when times were tough.

City officials were on the watch for the interest of the citizens, too. New ordinances were enacted, and the Clovis Fire Department continued to improve services. The area, like the nation, experienced rapid suburban growth in the post-war era and baby boom of the late 1940s and 1950s. To halt adjacent school districts from annexing newly developed subdivisions away from Clovis area schools, voters elected to unify, creating the Clovis Unified School District in 1959.

Members of the community helped each other through difficult times. From a period of challenges and sacrifice emerged an era of victory and recovery.

GRAPE PRICES REFLECT TIMES. When the 1919 Prohibition Amendment passed, the winemaking industry was thought to be in jeopardy. Growers throughout California removed vineyard acreage. The resulting crop scarcity drove up the price of grapes from $20 to over $200 per ton. By the time Prohibition was repealed in 1933, overplanting had forced the price down below the cost of production. Clovis vineyardist Fred Dawson (pictured) lived alone on his farm in Jefferson Colony during the week, while his wife resided in a Fresno apartment so their daughter could attend Fresno High School. Dawson's hard work and the high value of grapes provided a Mills College education and a Steinway piano for their daughter Ethel, which she used to help support her own young family by teaching piano during the Depression. (McFarlane Family Archive.)

AERIAL VIEW. In 1936, Clovis was a small town surrounded by farms. Once only open grain fields, settlers planted orchards and shade trees to provide income and respite from the intense summer heat. In the upper right, Tollhouse Road angles into Third Street, following the historic path of the flume. Visible on Fifth Street is the 1920 Clovis Union High School. (Clovis Unified School District.)

REFRESHING TIMES. Times were hard, but there was still time for refreshment with family and friends. Pictured in this undated photograph is White Front Café, located on Pollasky Avenue between Fourth and Fifth Streets. (Clovis Museum.)

FIRST GRADE. Shirley Pendergrass's 1930 first-grade class of 40 students reflects the growth in Clovis schools. Military buildings were moved from Lemoore Army Air Field and Hammer Field after World War II to add classroom space to the one-story brick Clovis Grammar School at Second and Pollasky Streets. The main building was condemned in 1952; students were divided between the new Luther Weldon and Sierra Vista Elementary Schools. (Ingmire-Bradley family.)

JEFFERSON ELEMENTARY. Many in Lena Clark's class of fifth- and sixth-graders rode to Jefferson Elementary School in a Model T bus. Principal Hazel Reyburn supervised class decorum to bolster Miss Clark, who was paid $1,400 annually. She recalled, "Those were depression days. Farmers were losing their land, raisins were worth very little, farm labor was paid 25¢ per hour." (McFarlane family archive.)

HALLOWELL SALES AND SERVICE. Dennis Hallowell's Studebaker and Texaco Service Station at Clovis and Fourth Avenues advertised in Clovis High School's 1940 Cavalcade yearbook, "gas, oil and repairing, washing, polishing, greasing; Phone 137." In 1950, Hallowell Chevrolet provided 24-hour towing service simply by dialing 4. The Hallowell family built up their dealership by selling Chevrolet vehicles to generations of valley residents. Other advertisers in the yearbook were Estill and Sunier Standard Oil Products, Dodge and Plymouth; C.M. Beasley Garage, De Soto and Plymouth Cars; H.B. Owens Chevrolet; Wayne Rall Ford, Mercury, Lincoln Zephyr and Shell Products; and Whiton's Cyclery. (Brett Hedrick.)

THE CLASS OF CHAMPIONS. In 1942, Clovis High School graduated an exceptional number of high-achieving students who went on to excel in many areas. Local sports legend Lloyd Merriman, pictured, excelled at football, basketball, and baseball throughout his high school career. He played baseball and football for Stanford University, then professional baseball with the Cincinnati Reds, the Chicago White Sox, and the Chicago Cubs. Agriculturalist Graydon Nichols's high school tennis foretold men's rankings of no. 1 nationally and no. 4 internationally in the 1980s. Louis Schramm, scouted by the St. Louis Cardinals, played for Victor McLaglen's farm team until he established his well drilling company. Col. Normand Biglione (US Army), a Korean War veteran, was comptroller of the Berlin Brigade in the 1960s. Frank Mesple was prominent in state politics and education. (Cincinnatti Reds Baseball Hall of Fame.)

GRADS HONORED. Graduates from Clovis High School have been recognized for their community contributions. Graduate Phillip Victor Sanchez, former Clovis Unified School District board trustee, became US ambassador to Honduras and Colombia. The CUSD McFarlane-Coffman Ag Center is named after two former trustees and advocates for the agriculture program, John Coffman and Bill McFarlane (1943). An elementary school is named for former CUSD trustee Bud Rank (1941).

RECRUITING BUS. World War II brought a call to Clovis High graduates to enlist in the American war effort. The US Army Recruiting Service bus (pictured above) at the corner of Fifth Street and Clovis Avenue (originally called Front Street and then Fulton Street until 1946) awaits new recruits. The original "Gateway to the Sierras" sign pictured here was first suspended over Clovis Avenue in 1930. (Clovis Museum.)

LUMBER IN TOWN. Bretz Mill operated near Shaver Lake in the late 1800s. Lumber was hauled to Clovis down Tollhouse Grade. A 1941 Bretz Bros. lumber company advertisement declares, "Manufacturers of Lumber from tree to building site." The Clovis Lumber Company advertised the following in 1941: "You can get complete building service, the finished job from basement to roof . . . Phone 6." (Clovis Chamber of Commerce.)

RAILS OF COMMERCE. The Clovis train station was a shipping center, bringing goods from far-off cities. During much of the 20th century, the railroad provided transportation for exports of lumber and agricultural products from a series of spurs and stops paralleling Clovis Avenue. After the original two-story station burned down, this single-story station was transported from Visalia to become the Clovis Depot.

A RICH HERITAGE. In 1913, Kehar Singh Brar, 17, and his brother, Dall Singh Brar, 24, left their village in the Punjab, India, on their journey to America. They worked with other Indian immigrants and accumulated savings. At that time, however, Indian immigrants were not permitted to purchase land. Eventually, the family lived and farmed at Bullard and Temperance Avenues, purchasing that 40-acre property from R.E.L. Good. It was not unusual to see Mrs. Brar working their land with a tractor. They are pictured here with their friend and neighbor, Frank McFarlane, age 90. Donning his familiar white turban, Brar was 74 at the time. His son Raj was five. Although the family name is Brar, they were widely known as Singh, a reference to their Sikh religion. (McFarlane family archive.)

As YOU leave your homes we wish to express our friendship for you and our belief in you as neighbors and fellow Americans. We would assure you that evacuation does not in our minds reflect in any way upon your integrity as citizens, and we do appreciate the fine spirit in which you are accepting this difficult situation.

* * *

Many of us know many of you personally, and are confident of your loyalty to the United States. Under the stress of this dislocation you are showing that loyalty in word and in spirit. We would have you feel this is only a temporary change and that after this unfortunate conflict is over you will be welcomed back to this Community and to your accustomed occupations of life.

* * *

We pledge ourselves to do everything possible to reduce the hazards and soften the effects of your enforced absence. We desire to help you, and thereby also help ourselves, to maintain the Christian spirit and the democratic way of life which we all love. We consider it a privilege to serve you in any way.

Our prayers and good will go with you, and if while you are away we can be of assistance to you in caring for your interests please call on us.

* * *

Your friends could not all have opportunity to endorse this message, but the undersigned represent them and assure you that they all gladly join us in this greeting.

CLOVIS COMMITTEE ON NATIONAL SECURITY AND FAIR PLAY

RALPH MASON DREGER,
Chairman, Pastor Methodist Church

FREDERICK V. DABOLD,
Pastor Baptist Church

PAUL E. ANDREW,
Principal Clovis Union High School

GLENN D. REAVIS,
Principal Clovis Elementary School

EBERT FRANCK,
President Chamber of Commerce

LUTHER E. WELDON,
Mayor City of Clovis

"A Message to Our Neighbors and Friends on the Day of Evacuation." Fumio Ikeda's family received this message signed by local Clovis leaders in July 1942 upon their internment at the Fresno Fairgrounds and prior to relocation out of state. Ikeda joined the US Army in 1941, serving with the Military Intelligence Service until 1945, when he was honorably discharged as a staff sergeant. (Mine Ikeda.)

A Gift of Friendship. Yoshibei Takahashi settled in Clovis in 1903, working as ranch foreman for Herbert G. Johnson. During the Japanese internment of World War II, widow Anna Johnson kept the Takahashi home safe while running her own farm and insurance agency. After repeal of the Alien Land Law, she deeded Yoshibei's son Yosh an acre of land as a wedding gift. (Takahashi family.)

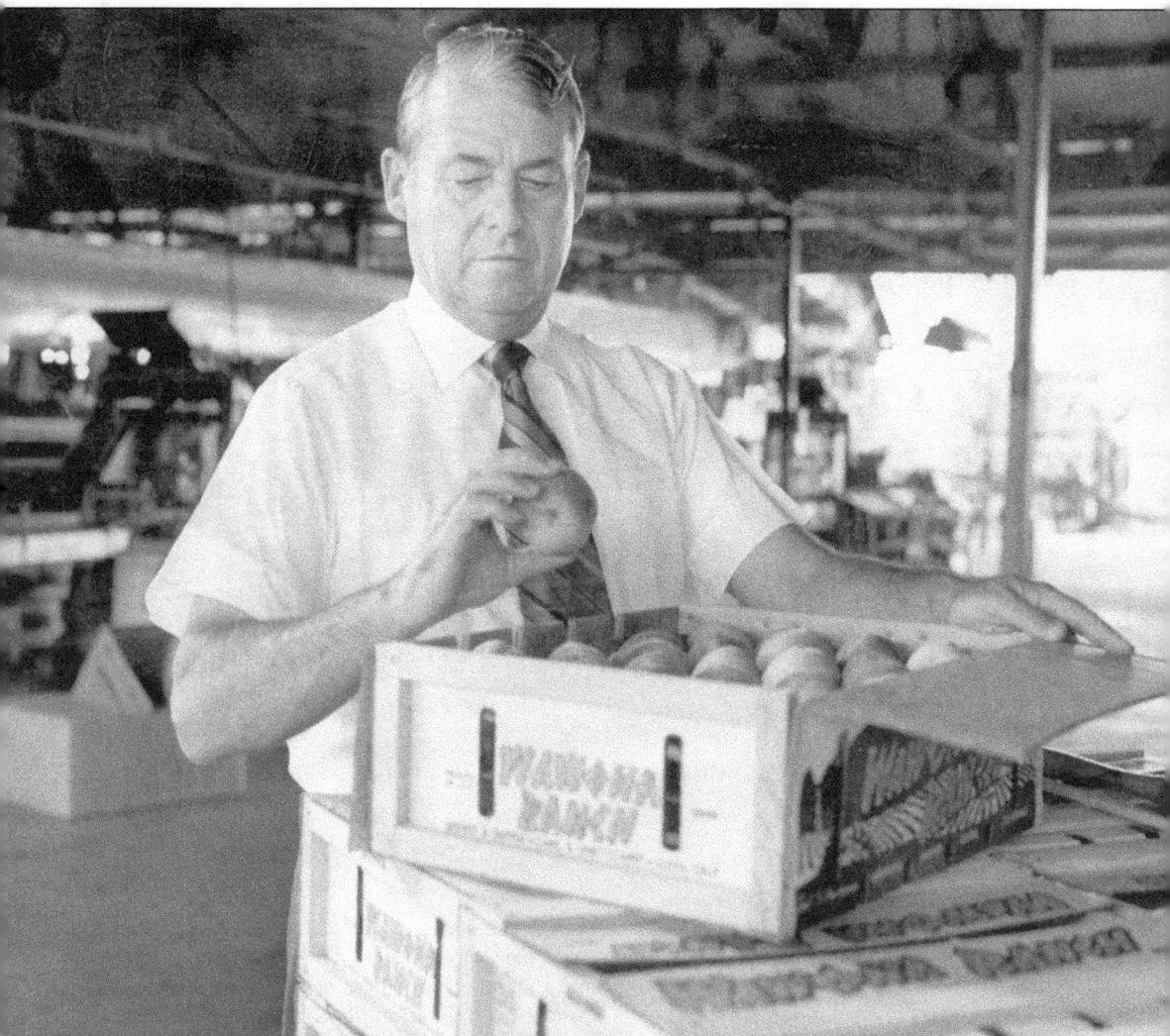

GROWING FARMLAND. The Takahashi farm at Herndon and Clovis Avenues was a local landmark for its produce stand and developed into a large open-air market. Kehar Brar farmed Wawona Ranch on Minnewawa Avenue for about 15 years until the opportunity arose to purchase the land. Brar was ineligible, so the 75-acre ranch was purchased by Robert Schmeiser in 1941. Son-in-law Earl Smittcamp, pictured, bought the property in 1945, then purchased neighboring properties in 40-acre increments. By 1960, the ranch had grown to 300 acres. Smittcamp opened a packinghouse in 1948 and marketed tree fruit on consignment. At its peak, the packinghouse represented 50 growers, packed 560,000 boxes annually, and hired 60 employees. The nearby railroad provided shipping. Citrus pioneer Gordon Harlan also benefited from a nearby rail spur. During the 1930s and 1940s, hundreds of immigrants from Mexico came to Clovis and worked at local ranches, including the Preuss ranch on Minnewawa. Pete Macias, born in Guadalajara, was foreman on the Balfe ranch and managed 1,000 acres. (Takahashi family; Smittcamp family.)

CLOVIS VETERANS MEMORIAL BUILDING OPENS. A December 1949 newspaper article states, "The memorial district, comprising Clovis, Friant and Pinedale, coincides with the area served by the Clovis Union High School, and derives its revenue from taxation of property in that area. The plans provide for a memorial building which will be available to fraternal and civic groups." The district formed on June 11, 1946. The first district directors included John B. Andreis, Ira Arbuckle, Carl S. Merriman, Carl Larson, and David E. Peckinpah. In April 1951, the building at Fifth and Hughes Avenues was completed. Pictured here, a ceremony of dedication to war veterans featured speaker Sam Hayes, radio commentator and Living Memorial Commission chairman, and representatives from American Legion and Veterans of Foreign Wars. Memorable gatherings included the mass immunization of school children against polio and other communicable diseases during the 1950s. (Clovis Veterans Memorial District.)

BOOMING BUSINESS. Postwar downtown business in Clovis enjoyed a period of rapid growth. Looking north from Pollasky and Fourth Streets, Cosby's clothing store, Valla's grocery, Clovis Stationery and Office Supply, Bank of America, and Carnegie Library face the Clovis Hotel. Dr. McMurtry's medical office and Deaver's Hardware are to the west. Looking east from the same intersection, Dr. Pendergrass's medical office, Evie Arnold's Clovis Florist and Loris Grossi's Clovis Cash Grocery face Rexall Drug to the north. At the end of the street sits the Southern Pacific train depot. A block to the south was the El Rey Theater, showing first-run movies. Grossi later changed the name of his market to Bad Boy. (Clovis Chamber of Commerce.)

MEDICAL SERVICES. Dr. Milton Scott McMurtry, widely known as Doctor Mac, began his practice in 1904 and served Clovis residents for more than five decades. A former 1896 home at 430 Pollasky Avenue, pictured, was converted into a sanitarium by the enterprising doctor. He made house calls, by horse and buggy or on foot, and later by automobile, and was an appointed physician for the Southern Pacific Railroad. Although it was a convenient downtown location for physicians and patients, the Clovis Sanitarium & Maternity Home was closed and demolished around 1960. The building had served the community through the postwar baby boom and Clovis was left without a hospital for several years until a funding drive was organized by local citizens to build a new and modern facility. Other principal physicians during this time were Dr. James E. Pendergrass and Dr. Wilbur Lose. Travis R. Pendergrass was the pharmacist at Clovis Drug Store, Inc. (Clovis Museum.)

PARADE BRINGS OUT TOWN. Pictured at right on April 28, 1956, in front of his office at 346 Pollasky Avenue, Dr. Milton McMurtry is accompanied by four little McFarlane girls whose births he had attended. They are watching the Clovis Rodeo Parade. The doctor's "shingle" hangs from the eave of the portico. His wife, Lucretia McMurtry, better known as Lu, chaired with Bessie Merriman the first Clovis Women's Club spring festival in 1914, later called the Clovis Day Festival in 1954. It became the Clovis Rodeo and Rodeo Parade. Pictured below, Wilbur Plaugher, arguably the most famous of all the celebrities who have participated regularly in the annual Clovis Rodeo, is a renowned rodeo clown and cowboy athlete who was inducted into the Rodeo Hall of Fame in Oklahoma City in 2007. (McFarlane Family; Wilbur Plaugher.)

Basket Weaver. Clovis area resident Tahubne Lena Walker, 1912–1979, was from the North Fork Mono tribe. She was called an "owl woman" because, when she was young, a great horned owl once walked with her. She was a master basket weaver and was the first to design an intricate diamond pattern weave. She served as "preparer and crier," preparing tribal families for news of a loved one's passing. (Ron Goode.)

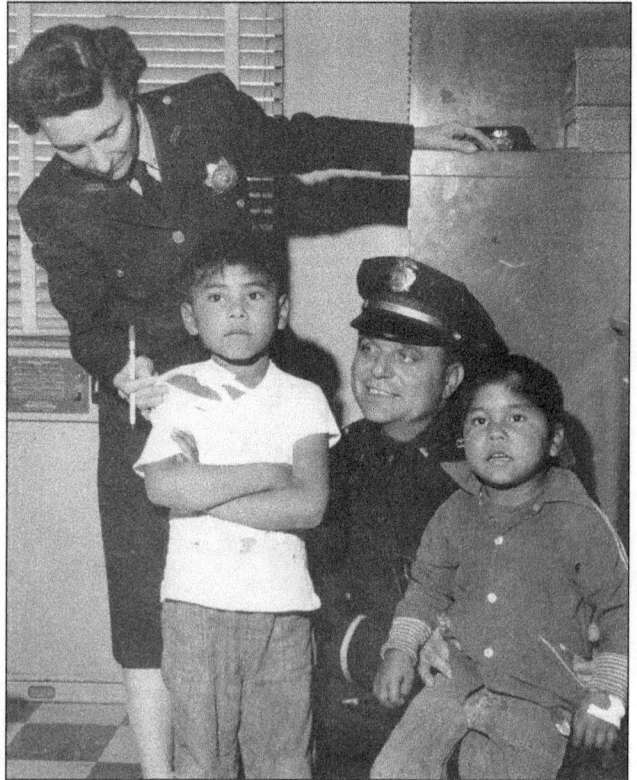

Dog Attacks. In 1960, wild dogs roved the Clovis streets and attacked five people. Stories ran in the local paper for weeks, including an article about the bites inflicted on Tony and Alvin Thomas, pictured with police officers Gino Pishione and Frances Qualls after receiving medical attention and affection from staff. The city recommended a census of dogs and an ordinance to monitor pet populations.

NEED FOR IMPROVED FIRE SERVICE. Even in the 1930s, fires were a constant threat to the safety of Clovis citizens. Improvements were constantly sought. Pictured above in 1935, fire chief Harry Whiton and crew mounted the "modern" Clovis Volunteer Fire Department engine. In 1952, a new fire station was constructed using volunteer labor, with materials furnished by the city. A 2,000-gallon water tanker was added to upgraded city fire services in 1959. Pictured below in 1961, an expanded Clovis Volunteer Fire Department posed in front of the Van Pelt engine. In 1962, six children of the Funk family died in a residential fire, despite efforts by neighbors and the volunteer fire department. As a result of this tragic event, the first official paid fire department was formed in 1966.

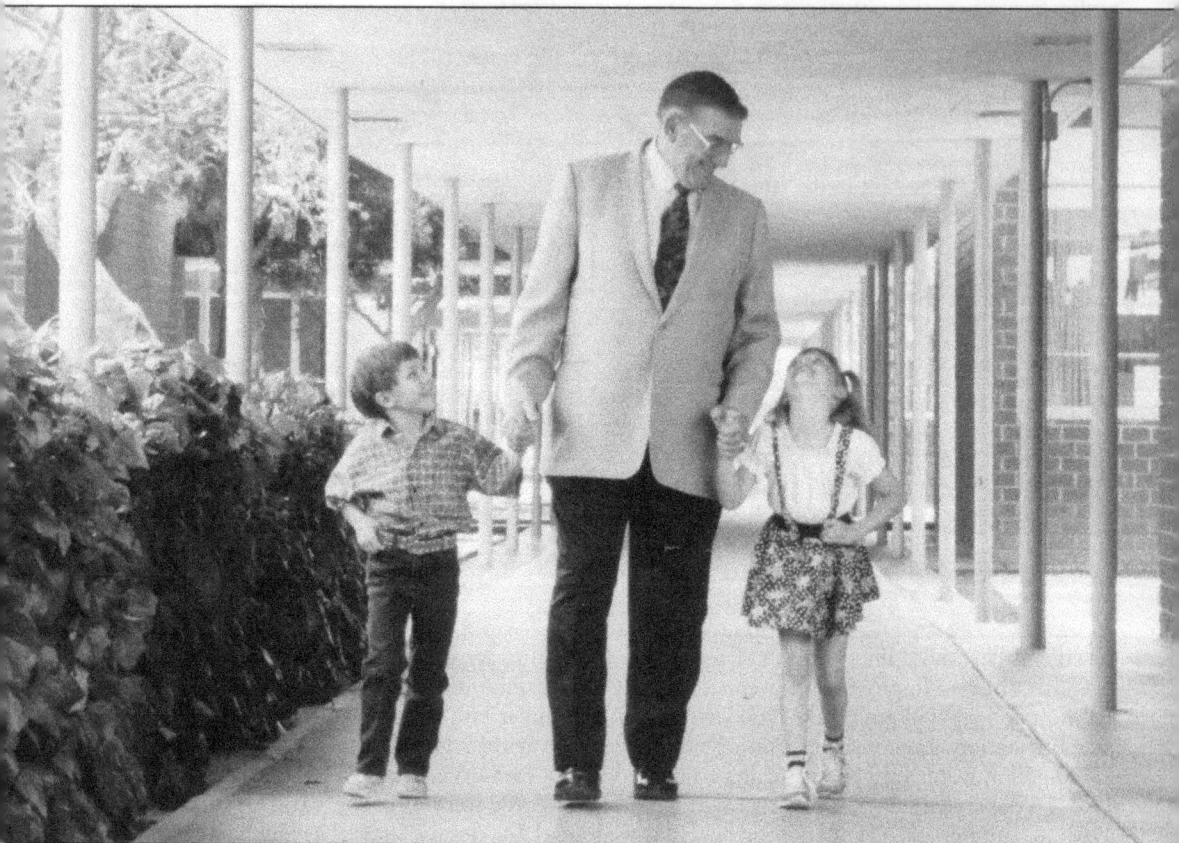

VISIONARY EDUCATOR. Floyd Buchanan arrived in Clovis in 1957 to interview for the position of superintendent of the Jefferson Union School District. A Walnut Creek principal, he was poised to receive his doctorate in education from University of California, Berkeley. Despite taxing dissertation work, he interviewed for the position. He met with the members of the school board at a table that was longer than the small room, sitting outside with a few of the trustees while the others sat inside. After the interview, he saw a distinguished man stepping out of a fine-looking automobile. As they departed, he said to his wife, Molly, "There goes our job." Yet, July 1957 found Dr. Buchanan employed with the small district, eager to remedy low reading and math skills that were causing high dropout rates in the upper elementary grades. In 1960, the newly formed Clovis Unified School District hired Buchanan as superintendent. He led the district for 31 years with his revolutionary Sparthenian concept for education of students well-rounded in mind, body, and spirit. (Clovis Unified School District.)

CLOVIS UNIFIED. In 1959, roughly 80 percent of Clovis voters elected to unify the districts of Temperance-Kutner, Jefferson, Tarpey, Cole, Sierra Vista, Fort Washington-Lincoln, Pinedale, Nelson, Dry Creek, Weldon, and Clovis High to form the Clovis Unified School District. In 1960, one trustee from each of the original districts comprised the new governing board, pictured above. Everett "Bud" Rank Jr. was the first president. (Clovis Chamber of Commerce.)

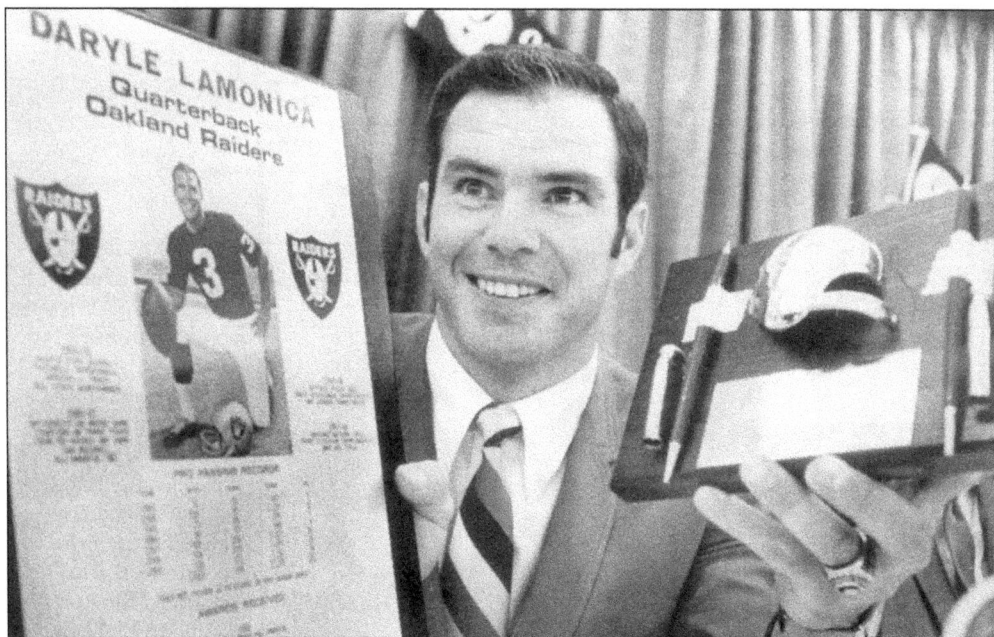

DARYLE LAMONICA. Clovis High School 1959 graduate and standout athlete Daryle Lamonica would go on to become starting quarterback at Notre Dame and later with the Oakland Raiders. He was named American Football League player of the year in 1967 and 1969. He played in the Pro Bowl and in the Super Bowl. Lamonica Stadium on Clovis High's campus is named in his honor. (Fresno Athletic Hall of Fame.)

85

COLD MUG. The end of an era came when the trees and grass of the park at the northeast corner of Clovis and Fifth Streets were replaced by an A&W Root Beer Drive-In, complete with roller-skating waitresses hanging food and drink-laden metal trays on car windows. The drive-in was one of the favorite hangouts of local high school students during the 1950s. (Clovis Museum.)

BAD BOY. Loris Grossi purchased Clovis Cash Grocery on Fourth Street in 1945. Because he extended customers credit while other grocers in town did not, he was called a "bad boy." He embraced the description and changed his store name to Bad Boy Market around 1947. Bad Boy Market relocated to Clovis Avenue in 1960. (Clovis Independent.)

Six

Decades of Growth
1960 to 2000

The first half-century of Clovis history was largely defined by agriculture and the city's proximity to the natural wealth of the Sierra Nevada. After World War II, an economic boom came to the area. The new Fresno State campus fostered the growth of surrounding neighborhoods. With the closing of Hammer Field (now Fresno Yosemite International Airport), the federal government gave Clovis 80 acres of land at Peach and Ashlan Avenues, including the sewer treatment plant. Addition of the treatment plant made land to the north more developable. Land was assembled, and annexations to Clovis began. As Fresno grew northward, homebuilders began to look for lower-priced land to meet the increasing demand for housing. Clovis staked a claim to the same areas, worried that Fresno's growth would overwhelm the city. The two cities fought lengthy court battles for parcels of land such as the area around Barstow and Willow Avenues. Entrepreneurs, seeing growth to the west, began establishing businesses along Shaw Avenue. During its second half-century, Clovis worked hard to welcome new growth without losing its small-town family values and sense of place. New families arrived. New schools opened. In order to accommodate a growing Fresno State student body, apartments were built in the area through the 1970s. As the city became more closely linked to the larger Fresno area, city leaders became concerned about maintaining the community's identity. Major efforts were undertaken to reinforce the heritage of Clovis. These efforts included revitalizing Old Town Clovis with a turn-of-the-century theme, developing regional shopping, building a new hospital, and attracting new industry. The city expanded its traditional Clovis Rodeo and began farmer's markets and other events to boost a sense of community. It has become nationally recognized for its many festivals. Clovis became a community of choice for many new residents coming to the San Joaquin Valley. It gained a well-earned reputation for quality education, excellent government services, and the "Clovis Way of Life."

BOUNDARIES SET. Fresno State began expansion of its new campus near Shaw and Cedar Avenues. There was little development in the area. The eastern boundary of the campus was Willow Avenue, which was also the eastern boundary of Fresno. Through legal actions between Fresno and Clovis, Willow ultimately became the legal boundary for future development in the two cities. (Hammer Field Collection, Special Collections, Madden Library, California State University, Fresno.)

HAMMER FIELD. In 1942, an airfield opened south of Clovis as a training base for the US Army Air Force during World War II. Hammer Field was later deactivated and, by 1949, was in civilian hands. One of the land transfers included 80 acres containing a sewer treatment plant to the City of Clovis. The plant supported future growth. (Hammer Field Collection, Special Collections, Madden Library, California State University, Fresno.)

HALLOWELL CHEVROLET'S BOLD MOVE. In 1965, James Hallowell made the visionary decision to move his car dealership from downtown Clovis to what many thought was the middle of nowhere. The new dealership was built at Shaw and Willow Avenues, where there were just empty fields at the time. Hallowell saw the growth in Fresno coming north and recognized that future growth would connect the two cities. There was a plan in place for the future 168 Freeway, which was finally constructed in 1999. In 1970, a Ford dealership located across the street from Hallowell's. Businesses continued to situate on prestigious Shaw Avenue. (Brett Hedrick.)

AFFORDABLE TRACT HOMES. Residential builders in the area were attracted to the southwest part of Clovis because of the sewer availability and the low cost of land. Subdivisions began to spring up in the area, such as the College Park subdivision. In 1966, a modest new home sold for $23,300. Ten years later, the average home price doubled to $46,200. (John Wright Collection.)

THE CITY EXPANDS. New homes in the southwest part of the city allowed many Clovis residents and newcomers to "live the American dream" of home ownership. Two of those early buyers, Harry Armstrong and Peg Bos, would go on to become mayors of the city. Pictured, homes near Gettysburg and Fowler Avenues are advertised in the 1980s starting at $59,950. (John Wright Collection.)

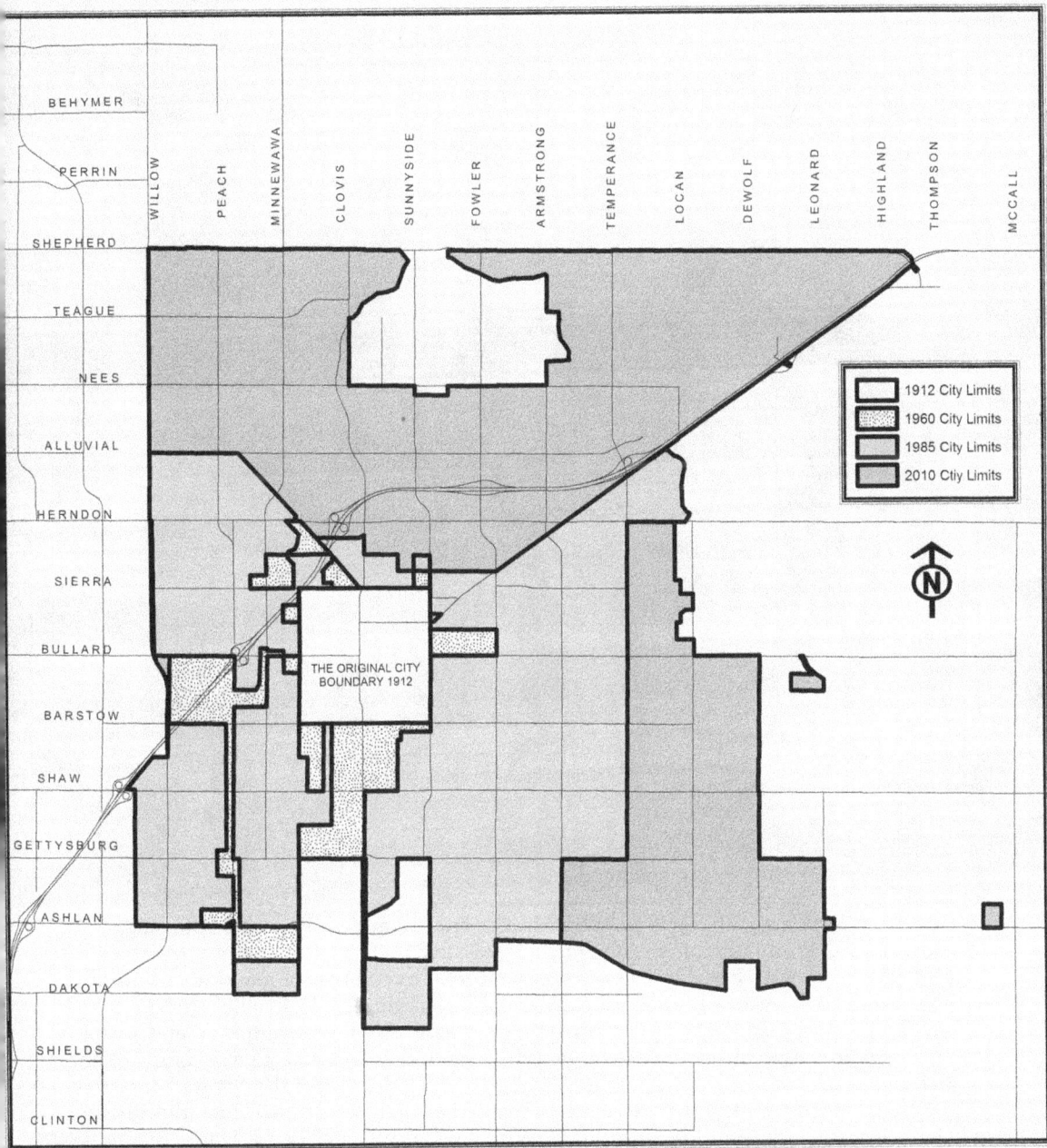

GROWTH TIMELINE. This city map shows the size of Clovis at different times. Shown are the original square-mile boundary and the city limits for 1960, 1985, and 2010. The unusual boundaries in the 1960s reflect several annexations to expand city services. (City of Clovis, Marianne Mollring.)

FIRST CITY MANAGER. The rapid growth of the city brought new administrative challenges. The Clovis City Council was concerned it might need more professional expertise to oversee the daily operations of the city. The decision was made to hire a full-time professional city manager. Prior to that time, each of the council members had oversight for one or more city departments such as fire, police, and public works. In 1971, the Clovis City Council hired Allen Goodman as Clovis's first city manager. Goodman, in turn, began hiring department heads for the finance and engineering departments, which increased the professionalism of the city staff. Goodman is pictured here with the 1972 city council. From left to right are (seated) Gene Papenhousen, Mayor Robert Estep, and John Antonio; (standing) Dennis Prindeville, Harry Armstrong, and Allen Goodman.

FIRST OFFICIAL CLOVIS CITY HALL. On the site of the original fire station, the city's first permanent city hall was located at Sixth and Pollasky Streets. The building housed the fire department, police department, and chambers for the city council. It also housed the city jail, whose occupants' noise would occasionally interrupt city council meetings. (Clovis Chamber of Commerce.)

A NEW CIVIC CENTER. Between 1970 and 1975, the population of Clovis almost doubled from 13,856 to 22,500 residents, creating a need for more city staff. By the early 1970s, the city outgrew city hall and added a temporary trailer to house planning and engineering departments. A new $2.1-million civic center was completed in May 1976. Some said the design "did not look Western enough." (John Wright Collection.)

NEW SCHOOLS. During the 1960s, Clovis Unified attendance grew an average of nearly five percent a year. In the 1950s, Clovis High's campus on Fifth Street had expanded to buildings across the street that would later become Clark Intermediate School. After observing an accident involving a school bus and a student, CUSD superintendent Dr. Floyd Buchanan spoke to the school board regarding moving the high school campus. A new campus would be located on 60 acres on Fowler and Barstow Avenues. The $4.1 million campus opened in 1969 with Peter G. Mehas as principal. This campus was followed by the district's second high school, Clovis West, in 1976. Three more high school campuses have since been added: Buchanan High School (1991), Clovis East (2000), and Clovis North (2007). Clovis Unified currently has 44 school sites.

REGIONAL SHOPPING MALL. In 1972, Fresno built Fashion Fair Mall, which drew shoppers out of Clovis. In 1978, city leaders saw the need for regional shopping in Clovis. A 57-acre site at the corner of Shaw and Clovis Avenues was selected for the project. The city met with owners, the McGarrys, and with a nationally recognized builder of retail centers, The Hahn Company. The builder liked the site and proposed a 500,000-square-foot center. Sierra Vista Mall opened in 1988. The mall was named Sierra Vista, drawing upon the city's historic "Gateway to the Sierras" theme. While the prospect of a regional center was exciting to many, downtown merchants worried it would spell the end of retail shops in downtown. In early 1980, the city embarked upon a plan for the revitalization of downtown Clovis. (John Wright Collection; City of Clovis.)

DOWNTOWN TO "OLD TOWN." In 1983, Clovis adopted a specific plan for downtown to reverse the trend of deterioration and vacancy that had plagued the area in the prior 20 years. A citizen's committee, under the guidance of planning director John Wright and city planner Jeff Witte, created a revitalization plan for the original square mile of Clovis. A new name was chosen for the area: Old Town Clovis.

THIS PROJECT IS IN CONJUNCTION WITH THE

CLOVIS COMMUNITY DEVELOPMENT AGENCY

AGENCY BOARD MEMBERS

Garry Woodward   Chairperson   Peggy Bos   Board Member

Tom Stearns   Pro–Tem   Marilyn Zygner   Board Member

Harry Armstrong   Board Member

For more information call 297–2340

A NEW DOWNTOWN STREETSCAPE. In 1987, plans for redevelopment of the streetscape began. All curbing, sidewalks, street surfaces, and signs in downtown were removed. During the renovation, businesses remained open. A turn-of-the-century design theme utilizing brick and cast iron was introduced as a way to mimic elements of the historical downtown. New public parking lots were also provided.

96

MANY HANDS. Successful redevelopment of Old Town Clovis was due to the dedication and involvement of the business community and city leaders. This group gathered in 1988 to celebrate the completion of the first phase of the streetscape. New brick and concrete sidewalks, landscape trees, cast-iron street lamps, and turn-of-the-century-style signage was installed, transforming the area into a vibrant retail and specialty shopping district. (John Wright Collection.)

RIBBON CUTTING. Mayor Garry Woodward joins, from left, planning director John Wright, council members Tom Stearns and Peg Bos, and city manager Ed Tewes in cutting the ribbon to celebrate the completion of the Old Town Clovis streetscape project. The evening included a festival complete with a reenactment of Western gunfights. Old Town Clovis is now recognized as an attractive retail and events destination. (John Wright Collection.)

MODERN DAY CLOVIS RODEO. In 2014, the Clovis Rodeo will mark its 100th year. World-champion cowboys and capacity crowds are drawn to the annual event held the last weekend in April. The Clovis Rodeo Association is a 700 member, volunteer nonprofit organization that raises money to benefit local charities and community groups.

FARMER'S MARKET IN OLD TOWN CLOVIS. The summertime Friday night farmer's market is sponsored by the Business Organization of Old Town. Booths offering fruits and vegetables for sale line Pollasky Avenue, while the music of live bands provides free entertainment. Special events such as the North American Pole Vault Championships and the annual peach party draw attendees to the market, which showcases the produce of the San Joaquin Valley.

WORLD-CLASS CYCLISTS IN CLOVIS. In 2009, one of the legs of the AMGEN Tour finished in Old Town Clovis to an enthusiastic crowd. The high caliber of winners crossing the finish line reflected the level of national events attracted to the city.

BALLOONS OVER CLOVIS. As part of the annual ClovisFest two-day celebration in the fall, hot-air balloons rise over the city during the early morning hours. The Clovis Chamber of Commerce, which incorporated in 1930 to act as a resource and support for the business community, sponsors ClovisFest. It also sponsors Big Hat Days, which kicks off rodeo month, and it supports community festivals, street fairs, and community leadership training.

LONGEST-SERVING COUNCIL MEMBER. First elected to the city council in 1970, Harry Armstrong will have served for 42 years when Clovis celebrates its centennial in 2012. He is the longest continually serving elected official in the state of California and served as mayor of Clovis five times.

CLOVIS FIRSTS. In 1974, Peggy M. Bos became the first woman appointed to the Clovis Planning Commission; in 1978, she was the first woman elected to the Clovis City Council; and in 1984, she was the first woman named mayor of Clovis. Raised in Clovis, she has served in numerous community organizations and as the president of the Clovis–Big Dry Creek Historical Society.

FREEWAY 168. Freeway 168 was included in plans for the valley in 1956, far in advance of its need. It was almost abandoned in the 1980s when Gov. Jerry Brown declared an end to California freeway construction. The Clovis City Council voted to keep it in the city's General Plan. Construction became a reality in 1999. Clovis politician Harry Armstrong led the effort to construct it. (John Wright Collection.)

TARPEY DEPOT RESTORATION. This original railroad depot was once located on the southeast corner of Ashlan and Clovis Avenues. Built in 1891 by the San Joaquin Valley Railroad, it has also served as a schoolhouse, post office, winery office, and real estate office for Tarpey Village. The building was moved to Fourth and Clovis Avenues in 1998, restored, and now serves as the Clovis Tourist Information and Visitors Center.

101

NEW HOSPITAL OPENING IN CLOVIS. In December 1988, Clovis Community Hospital opened a new $32-million medical center as part of a larger medical campus site near Temperance and Herndon Avenues. Orange orchards surround the medical towers and office suites that serve the expanding community. Previously, patients in Clovis were treated at the Clovis Memorial Hospital facility on DeWitt Avenue built in 1965. (Norm Andrews.)

NEW TECHNOLOGY. It was lifelong resident Einar Cook's Scandinavian heritage that connected him with Denmark and Poul Due Jensen, owner of Grundfos Pumps. When Grundfos decided to expand to North America, Cook sold them on his hometown as the location for their new manufacturing facility. The Center for Advanced Research and Technology (CART) occupies the former Grundfos site today at Clovis and Santa Ana Avenues.

INDUSTRY LEADER. To create employment in the community, the city developed its own business park on the old Hammer Field property in the 1980s south of Ashlan at Peach Avenue. PELCO, a world-renowned video and security systems manufacturer, occupies most of the business park today and is Clovis's largest private employer. PELCO was purchased by Snyder Electric in 2007.

"FROM OUR FAMILY TO YOURS." Embracing the family values and heritage of Clovis, Anlin Industries came to the city in 1999. In 2000, the company received the Small Business Administration's "Small Business of the Year" award. The state-of-the-art window and door manufacturer is dedicated to its employees and also often displays patriotic decorations and holiday messages at its Tollhouse and Fowler Avenues plant.

103

RAILS TO TRAILS. In 1997, the City of Fresno and the City of Clovis bought sections of the abandoned Southern Pacific Railroad right-of-way for $3.5 million to create a biking and pedestrian pathway. It was to be the flagship of a trail system that would run throughout the metropolitan area. On May 6, 2000, nearly 3,000 community volunteers planted 4,800 trees on eight miles of the trail in the remarkable time of 2 hours and 56 minutes. A system of trails, including the Old Town Trail, Dry Creek Trail, and Enterprise Canal Trail in Clovis, has become a treasured amenity in the community. Clovis planning director John Wright and Mark Keppler, the chairman of the Coalition for Community Trails, were recognized by the Clovis Hall of Fame in 2000 for their leadership in establishing the trails. (John Wright Collection.)

Seven

CLOVIS IN THE 21ST CENTURY
2000 TO 2011

Two challenges faced Clovis at the beginning of the 21st century. One proved to be a hollow threat, the other very real. Y2K, the computer disaster forecast to occur at midnight January 1, 2000, never materialized, but the terrorist strike on September 11, 2001, embedded itself in the minds of all Americans and significantly shaped the decade. The start of 2000 brought great economic prosperity in a near-unprecedented building boom. The decade brought hundreds of millions of dollars in new public facilities to meet the needs of a rapidly expanding community. The city population grew from 70,000 to nearly 97,000 in 10 years. A new surface-water treatment plant was built on the historic Enterprise Canal, providing water to supplement city wells. A new sewer treatment plant and new city corporation yard were constructed. Two new fire stations were also built. In addition, Clovis Unified School District opened two new educational centers, Clovis East (2000) and Clovis North (2007). Because of ongoing community support of special bond measures and a belief in high standards of school facilities and programs, CUSD continued to earn national recognition for excellence. Few could have imagined at the start of this decade of great prosperity that the city soon would be facing some of the most severe budgeting challenges in its 100-year history. The economic recession, foreclosures, and unemployment were to become familiar terms in many families. As in times gone by, the city and citizens are working together to meet the challenges. An enthusiastic task force is meeting to update the city's General Plan, putting together a vision of Clovis for the future that supports the community's core values and lays a road map to recovery. Clovis has much to celebrate as it approaches its centennial anniversary. Clovis remains a steadfast community of people who are willing to roll up their sleeves in order to build a quality way of life for now and for generations yet to come.

WE MUST NEVER FORGET. "The tragic events of September 11, 2001, were for most Americans a profound call to action. . . . We have all been brought closer together by our common losses and collective grief. We have been reminded of how uniquely fortunate we are to live in the greatest country in all of history; where liberty and justice are the very cornerstones of our lives. We have learned not to take for granted our men and women in uniform—those who stand ready to risk their lives protecting the rest of us. We now know who the real heroes are," said PELCO executive David L. McDonald at the 2002 opening of the California Memorial Museum on the PELCO business campus honoring the heroes of 9/11. Buchanan Educational Center's Veterans Stadium was named such following 9/11 to honor all heroes from Clovis who gave their lives in service to their country. Since 9/11, at the time of this writing those include Jeremiah Baro, Jared Hubbard, Anthony Butterfield, Rowen Walter, Nathan Hubbard, Nicholas Eischen, Brian Piercy, Matthew Abbate, Raymond Mendoza-Mathews, Steven Packer, and Michael Rojas.

CLOVIS VETERANS MEMORIAL BUILDING ADDITIONS. The Veterans Memorial Building was renamed in 1984 Rex Phebus Veterans Memorial Building in honor of Phebus and his 30 years as its district manager. In 2007, the building underwent extensive remodeling to add modern offices, meeting rooms, banquet facilities, and a 350-seat auditorium. (John Wright Collection.)

MILITARY MEMORIAL. At the Rex Phebus Veterans Memorial Building on Hughes Avenue are statues of five figures standing in a semicircle around the boots, rifle, and helmet of a fallen comrade. Each figure represents a military branch from an era of American history. The sculptor, Thomas King, completed the memorial in 2003.

STYLISH "HOUSE." Nearly one in four residents moved to Clovis in the first decade of the 21st century. The city undertook an unprecedented public works construction campaign, including a new sewer pump station at Ashlan and Leonard Avenues. During construction of the stylishly disguised pump house, pictured, several people stopped and asked where they could get plans for the "house," wanting to build the same plan.

WATER FOR PEOPLE. In 2006, a new surface-water treatment plant was built on the historic Enterprise Canal. Once again, this pioneering water canal would make possible the continued expansion of the community of Clovis. The facility dramatically reduced the city's dependence on groundwater that had been its sole source of drinking water.

INVESTING IN THE COMMUNITY. In 1999, the voters of Clovis approved a $15-million public safety bond measure. The measure funded the construction of a new police and fire administration building that was completed in 2003. The facility, located at 1233 Fifth Street, included a modern jail. The city had been without its own jail since the new civic center opened in 1976. (John Wright Collection.)

EXPANDING SERVICES. Fire Station No. 1 opened in 2008 at Pollasky and Seventh Streets. One of two new fire stations funded by the 1999 public safety bond, it replaced the outdated fire station located at the same corner. The design for the front doors was inspired by the 1918 Clovis Grammar School.

109

CHANGES AT THE MALL. In 2006, Sierra Vista Mall underwent a major renovation adding a new megaplex theater, retail shops, and restaurants surrounding a central plaza. Live jazz band music and community booths fill the plaza during the summer music series "Rock the Mall."

THE AVENUE. The Clovis Chamber of Commerce, the City of Clovis, and Shaw Avenue merchants undertook a marketing and improvement program for Shaw Avenue, the city's principal retail street, naming it "The Avenue." An eclectic variety of shops extend from Armstrong Avenue to the 168 Freeway at Willow Avenue. (John Wright Collection.)

HIGH-TECH BLOOMS IN CLOVIS. In 2001, the City of Clovis broke ground on the Research and Technology Park in northeast Clovis to draw technology businesses to Clovis. Clovis envisions an innovative technology hub, to be known in the region for its entrepreneurial spirit, interest in education, and willingness to look beyond the horizon. Pictured are Shawn Miller, Harry Armstrong, Mike Dozier, and Art Reker.

PLACES TO PLAY. Near Old Town Clovis, Treasure Ingmire Park was one of the first municipal parks. Since then, 10 new city parks have been added as well as numerous neighborhood parks. Pictured at Clovis and Alluvial Avenues is Dry Creek Park, which offers play structures and an adjacent walking and biking trail. (John Wright Collection.)

CLOVIS RESIDENTIAL BOOM. The first decade of the 21st century saw a major residential building boom of 10,000 new homes. Some prospective homebuyers camped overnight at sales offices for a chance to purchase a home. Lotteries were held for prime building lots, and construction was booming. The 2008 economic crisis halted the boom and brought serious consequences to many valley residents. (John Wright Collection)

PLANS FOR THE FUTURE. As Clovis passes its centennial year, the growing city continues to develop ways to deliver a small-town feel. The Loma Vista planned community in southeast Clovis, pictured, is an example of an urban center with walking paths connecting residential neighborhoods and schools harkening back to the friendly neighborhoods of historic Clovis. Future plans include a community center with a village green. (John Wright Collection.)

Eight

A JOURNEY THROUGH TIME

One of the strengths of a great community is found in the knowledge of its past. The "then and now" images in this chapter are a journey through time that connect those who live in and visit Clovis today with the rich heritage of our city's dynamic past. In these images, streetscapes evolve from dirt roads lined with wooden walkways to newly paved roads illuminated by modern electric lighting. The horse and buggy is replaced with the Model T and later by modern cars parked near burgeoning Old Town Clovis businesses. Architectural changes reflect styles of specific decades and the economic climate of the times. With the changes, however, Clovis still reflects its turn-of-the-century heritage in many of its buildings.

Change is inevitable. But how a community changes has a great deal to do with how residents see their hometown. Clovis residents, past and present, clearly cherish this community. Clovis was built out of the dreams of early pioneers looking to provide for their families. Together they created a way of life that continues to be embraced today. Knowledge of Clovis history and an understanding of the dynamic changes that have occurred over time may offer a clearer perspective of the community as Clovis moves forward into and beyond its centennial year.

FIRST HOSPITAL. In the 1920s, Dr. Milton S. McMurtry established the Clovis Sanitarium as a local hospital. One of the two magnolia trees still stands at the original location of the hospital at 430 Pollasky Avenue. (Clovis Museum.)

MODERN HOSPITAL. In 1988, the new Clovis Community Hospital opened on its Temperance and Herndon Avenues campus, surrounded by acres of orange groves. Medical office construction has since improved the campus, and in 2013 the Clovis Community Medical Center is scheduled to open its $300-million expansion, doubling the size of the previous hospital. (John Wright Collection.)

EARLY FIRE STATION. Fire chief Harry Winton stands outside the only city fire station in 1935. Also pictured are Cliff DeSoto, Oliver Crocker, a young Harry Rogers, and Jack Kurty. Note the corrugated metal on the fire station exterior.

STATE-OF-THE-ART FIRE STATION. The Clovis Fire Station No. 5 at Alluvial and Temperance Avenues houses 21st-century equipment. Note the corrugated metal design on the firehouse.

HOBLITT HOTEL. Pictured is the landmark hotel under construction in 1902 at Pollasky and Fourth Streets. (Clovis Chamber of Commerce.)

HOTEL BECOMES LILLIE FRANCES. The Hoblitt Hotel became the Lillie Frances, pictured in the 1920s. Fire destroyed the top floor of the hotel on August 10, 1927.

RECONSTRUCTED HOTEL. The lower two floors survived the 1927 fire and were remodeled for use as offices and small business space as well as apartments on the second floor. This photograph was taken around 1970.

RESTORATION. Griff Ashurst purchased the property in 1977 and later renovated the building, housing the Clovis Community Development Agency office upstairs and the Victoria Rose restaurant on the ground floor. (John Wright Collection.)

117

EARLY CLOVIS. This c. 1910 Clovis postcard looks north on Pollasky Avenue from Fifth Street. The three-story Hoblitt Hotel can be seen in the distance on Fourth Street. (John Reynolds Collection.)

C.F. SELLERS BUILDING. This c. 1915 photograph shows the northeast corner of Pollasky and Fifth Streets, now called the C.F. Sellers building. The DeWitt Building is to the north, and the J.E. Good building can be seen on the right. The false front of the building is concealed by the large trees. (Clovis Museum.)

FIRE CLAIMS THE SECOND FLOOR.
In 1930, fire swept through the
second floor of the Frank Arminiso
Building at the northeast corner of
Pollasky and Fifth Streets. At that
time, a dance hall occupied the
second floor. The DeWitt Building
can again be seen to the north.

TODAY. This 2011 photograph shows the surviving first floor of the building at the northeast corner of Pollasky and Fifth Streets, which was remodeled. The DeWitt Building located to the north was torn down for structural safety reasons and replaced with retail and restaurant space. The DeWitt Building's granite sign stands on the sidewalk between the two buildings. (John Wright Collection.)

FRONT STREET. The J.E. Good General Merchandise Building can be seen on the left side of this c. 1912 photograph looking north on Front Street (now Clovis Avenue) from Fifth Street. (John Reynolds Collection.)

FULTON STREET. Front Street was for a while called "Fulton Street," after the railroad promoter Fulton G. Berry, whose name is carried on Fulton Street in Fresno. This 1939 photograph was taken after the first paving of the street in 1922. The street was later renamed Clovis Avenue.

CLOVIS AVENUE. This 1970s image shows Clovis Avenue prior to the Old Town Streetscape renovations. The old A&W Root Beer Drive-In at the northeast corner of Clovis Avenue and Fifth Street is on the right.

OLD TOWN CLOVIS AVENUE. Clovis Avenue at Fifth Street continues to be the heart of the city. This 2011 photograph shows the renovated streetscape and building fronts that draw upon historical Clovis architecture. Old Town has strict design guidelines to maintain the theme of the area. (Michael K. Fennacy.)

CARNEGIE LIBRARY. The library opened in 1914 on Pollasky Avenue north of Fourth Street as one of the many across the nation funded by Andrew Carnegie. It served the community until the mid-1970s. (Clovis Museum.)

CHAMBER OF COMMERCE BUILDING. As the community approaches its centennial anniversary, the Chamber of Commerce occupies the Carnegie Library building, where it continues to promote and protect small businesses. (John Wright Collection.)

CLOVIS GRAMMAR SCHOOL. Romanesque Revival architecture was the theme for the grammar school's design in 1918. The building was torn down in 1956 because of structural safety concerns. (Fresno County Public Library.)

REFLECTING THE PAST. The front doors of Clovis Fire Station No. 1, which was built in 2008, reflect the architectural design of the 1918 Clovis Grammar School pictured above. The design concept for the building was drawn by then city planner Dwight Kroll. The city's 1936 fire truck is shown parked in front of the station.

THE WALKING DOCTOR. Starting in 2006, the city began installing public artwork along the Old Town Trail to develop the Heritage Walk. The trail is now dotted with life-size, bronze statues. *The Walking Doctor*, on Third Street, east of Clovis Avenue, pays tribute to former town doctors and their dedication to the community. The Pendergrass family of doctors was the inspiration for the statue.

THE TIES THAT BIND. The image of a father bending to tie his young son's shoe represents the family values that have always been an integral part of the Clovis community. This statue is located on the Heritage Walk along the trail on Fifth Street, east of Clovis Avenue. Other trail artwork includes *Bronco Buster* at Sierra and Clovis Avenues and the *Acorn Gatherer* on Shaw and Clovis Avenues.

Solid Leadership. The 2011 city council members are, from left to right, Nathan Magsig, Harry Armstrong, Lynne Ashbeck, Mayor Jose Flores, and Bob Whalen. Before there was a city council, Clovis was governed by a board of trustees, led by a president. The presidents were L.W. Gibson (1912), E.C. Smallin (1918), and O.L. Russell (1926). Past mayors of Clovis include James E. Pendergrass (1928), F.A. Hill (1931), E.E. Kenneaster (1931), T.R. Pendergrass (1932), J.W. Bittle (1934), L.W. Owens (1936), C.A. Booher (1938), Luther E. Weldon (1940), Wayne Rall (1948), John B. Weldon (1956), Douglas Dresser (1958), Carl McDonald (1963), John Antonio (1965), Glenn D. Reavis (1966), John I. Polson (1968), Ralph Joseph (1970), Robert E. Estep (1972), Dennis Prindiville (1974 and 1980), Stanley E. King (1976 and 1984), Gene Papenhausen (1978), Harry Armstrong (1982, 1990, 1994, 1999, and 2009), Peggy Bos (1984), Garry Woodward (1986), Tom Stearns (1988), Dave Lawson (1992), Patricia Wynne (1997), Jose Flores (2001 and 2011), Lynne Ashbeck (2003), Nathan Magsig (2005), and Bob Whalen (2007). Clovis's four city managers have been Allen Goodman, Ed Tewes, Kathy Millison, and Rob Woolley.

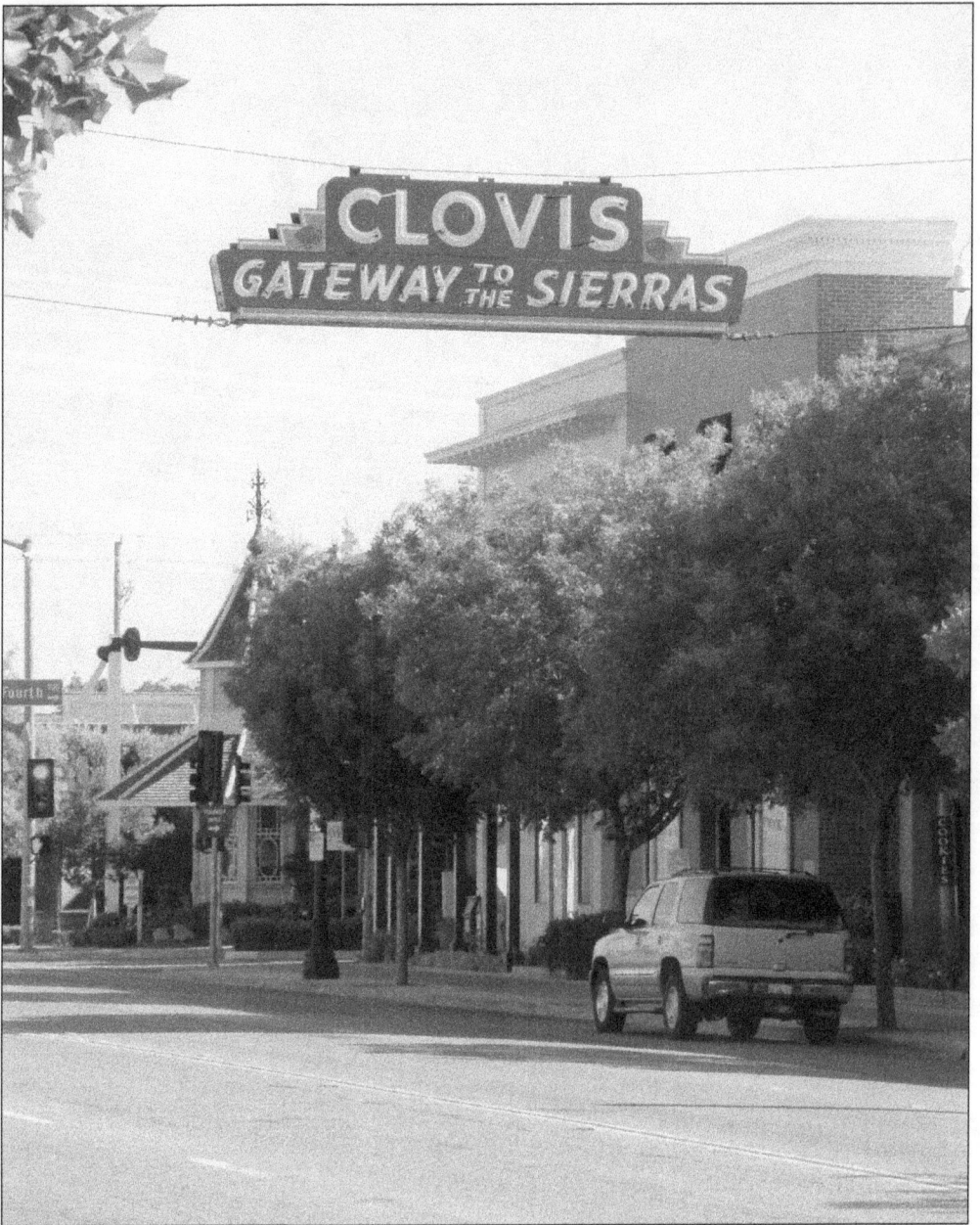

GATEWAY TO THE SIERRAS. The iconic sign suspended over Clovis Avenue between Fourth and Fifth Streets was first installed by the Chamber of Commerce in 1930 and was made of wood. The sign first established the misspelling of Sierra, adding an S to the end. Though the misspelling was acknowledged by the community, it has been preserved in successive versions of the sign. The original sign was replaced by a metal sign in 1946 and again in 1951 with the present-day metal and neon-lit version. The sign was taken down and restored in 1992 in a community effort led by lifelong residents Fred and Suzie Osterberg. The neon sign continues to signify Clovis's deep connection to the Sierra Nevada. The sign evokes memories of early days, when ambitious lumbermen and entrepreneurial pioneers together established a small town, essentially where the sign now hangs. (John Wright Collection.)

126

BIBLIOGRAPHY

50 Unified Years: Building a Tradition of Excellence in Clovis Unified Before, During and After Unification. Compiled by Susan Sawyer Wise with Kelly Avants, watercolors by Pat Hunter. Fresno, CA: produced by Clovis Unified School District in conjunction with Craven Streets Books, 2011.

Atkin, William T. *The History of Clovis: 50 Years of Progress*. Edited by Malcolm Johnson. Clovis, CA: 1962.

Clovis Independent. *Celebrating One Hundred Years Together: The Clovis Independent March 1905–2005*. Clovis, CA: 2005.

Chedister, Arthur W. *The Story of Clovis*. Clovis, CA: 1954.

Clovis Diamond Jubilee Committee. *Clovis, California, 75th Anniversary, 1912–1987*. Clovis, CA: The Committee, 1980.

Clovis Independent and Tribune. *The Clovis Independent & Tribune 75th Anniversary Special Issue: Past, Present & Future of Clovis*. Clovis, CA: 1980.

Clovis Tribune. Clovis, CA: H.E. Armstrong and Sons, 1905–1942.

Early Days in Clovis. Compiled by Clovis Adult Education. Clovis, CA: Clovis Unified School District, 1976.

Fresno-Clovis Metropolitan Area Project. *A Profile of the Population and Housing in the Fresno-Clovis Metropolitan Area*. Prepared by the Planning and Public Works Departments of the City and County of Fresno, CA; report supervision, Neil C. Gustafson. Fresno, CA: 1964.

Fresno Guide. *Fresno Guide Presents the History of Clovis*. Clovis, CA: 1979.

Howison, Thomas. *The Story of My Life: Personal Remembrances of Over Ninety Years*. Fresno, CA: Pioneer Pub, 1981.

Images of an Age, Clovis: A Sharing of Reminiscences, Illustrations and Photographs of the Historical Development of the Clovis Community, Its People, Schools, Organizations, Churches and Its Surrounding Rural Areas. Fresno, CA: Pacific Printing Press, 1984.

Visit us at
arcadiapublishing.com